S w a m i   S e z

Trade
The
Blues
For
Brownies!™

365 Days and Over 365 Ways
Guide to Happiness
and
Spiritual Enlightenment
(with Daily Affirmations... plus Jokes !!)

BEYOND "CHICKEN SOUP FOR THE SOUL"
EASIER TO DECIPHER THAN "THE DA VINCI CODE"

S w a m i   S e z

Trade
The
Blues
For
Brownies!™

365 Days and Over 365 Ways
Guide to Happiness
and
Spiritual Enlightenment
(with Daily Affirmations... *plus Jokes !!*)

Bruce E. Singer aka Swami Sez

Swami Sez Press
United States of America

Swami Sez Press
a division of We Publish Books
P.O. Box 1814
Rancho Mirage, CA 92270

www.SwamiSezPress.com
E-mail: SwamiSezPress@gmail.com

Library of Congress Cataloging in Publication

Bruce E. Singer/ Swami Sez Trade The Blues For Brownies

Printed in the United States and London

Swami Sez Trade The Blues For Brownies / by Bruce E. Singer

SEL004000 SELF HELP / Affirmations
HUM000000 HUMOR / General
PSY049000 PSYCHOLOGY / Depression

ISBN-10: 1929841-33-7 Paperback
ISBN-13: 978-1-929841-33-2 Paperback

First Printing 2006

Swami Sez Press

Swami Sez:

"Trade the Blues for Brownies!"

- Includes 365 days and over 365 ways to "Beat the Blues"
- Experience the Ultimate Self-Help / Humor Journal
- Words of Wisdom / Daily Affirmations
- "Depression Buster" Guide to a Better Day
- Transform your "Ah! Ha's!" into "Ha! Ha's!!"

What they would say if they were so inclined...or if they were Robert Klein:

"Sure I love Chicken Soup...but there's NOTHING like trading the blues for brownies."   *– Jack Canfield*

"An instant classic! Definitely easier to decipher than the DaVinci Code."   *– Dan Brown*

"There's no time like NOW for some great Swami Sez humor and affirmations."   *– Eckhart Tolle*

"Swami's humor is transformational...your Id, Ego and Super Ego will thank you!!"   *– Sigmund Freud*

"I would say that 'Trade the Blues for Brownies' is like a dream come true."   *– Carl Jung*

"I gave my copy of 'Swami Sez' to Paul Shaffer...have you seen his smile lately??"   *– David Letterman*

"Swami takes over where Carnac left off...where do you think I get my material??"   *– Jay Leno*

"After I watch last night's re-run of *The Tonight Show,* I always write something funny in the 'Idea Of the Day' section of my 'Swami Sez' journal. Thanks to Swami Sez and good fortune, I'll be the new host of *The Tonight Show.*"   *– Conan O'Brien*

humor/wisdom/satire/parody

What Is an Affirmation?

AN AFFIRMATION
(from Latin: affirmare)
means to assert that something is true
(The Constitution of the United States
makes four references to affirmations)

In personal or spiritual development
an affirmation is a form of autosuggestion
in which a statement of a desirable intention or condition
is deliberately repeated or meditated on
in order to implant the affirmation in the mind
so that the *new* thought can replace
the *previous* with the new *desirous*

Scientifically through repetition of affirmations
the neocortex can supercede the supposed dominant subcortex
(Don't worry about it... leave it to the scientists)

Just know that affirmations can be like MIRACLES
(and they work if you work them !!)

As you will see, affirmations are a very powerful means of
reprogramming the unconscious mind...
These 366 positive affirmations are most effective when repeated
in a quiet and relaxed state:
Use the Swami Magic Breathing Technique
'4 ~ 7 ~ 8'
Breathe in to the count of 4 — hold for 7
Breathe out to the count of 8 — then repeat

The following are two of the most "true to the core" known affirmations
(which also happen to contain a rhyme to make them more memorable)

"Every Day in Every Way. . . I Am Getting Better and Better"
By Dr. Emile Coué
Father of Autosuggestion

And then the foundation of them all:
When the individual accepts self-responsibility for his or her own life
"If It Is to Be. . . It Is Up to Me"
By Dr. Ernest Holmes
Founder of Science of Mind

Yet, the most often used and well-known affirmation is the word
"*Amen*" which can be translated simply "*So be it* " or "*So mote it be*"
setting into motion the truth of whatever was just written or said.
Amen

How To Get The Most From This Book

First, start right from where you are: *the ever-present...NOW!!*

THIS BOOK IS INTENDED TO BE NO LESS THAN A MIRACLE !!!

Just one idea contained within these pages can change your world... positively

To begin, turn to today's date and read Swami's message for the day
Next, turn to the page of your birth date ...and read your birth day message
Now ask Swami, "What other *ANSWERS* do you have that I need to know?"
Close your eyes and open to a page at random...
You have just experienced a mighty *Swami "Ah! Ha!"* or a hilarious *"Ha! Ha!!"*
Now turn your attention to today's Daily Affirmation...
To get the best results, keep repeating this affirmation as you stare at it
until it becomes like a "3-D hologram in your mind"
Best results occur by memorizing each affirmation and repeating it morning and night
(Hey, if you've got the blues... you gotta' do *something!!*)
Oh, and eating a brownie while reading this book can also be quite excellent *!!!*

Swami Insight:

Whether the print be large, medium or small face
the deeper answer exists . . . between the space

For maximum benefit, *repeat* today's affirmation 7 times in a row, 3 times a day:
This "locks it in" to your mind, allowing the "higher mind"
to *"MANIFEST WHAT YOU DESIRE"* over *"WHAT IS"*

This is a life-changing awareness:

Your Mind Can Make You Well... Right Here, Right Now!!

Remember to write something in your book everyday:
(even if it's just creative scribbling or doodles)
For the ultimate experience, use a carbon pencil
(available at your local art supply store)
Since it's carbon...and WE'RE carbon...
the pencil and you actually are one and the same
Whatever you write then... is YOU... And YOU... are it... Try it...it's magic*!*

A Good Idea:

Make this your personal idea book and creative journal
Take this book with you wherever you go...
on vacation, by your bed, in the car, on the train,
over hill, over dale... as we hit the dusty trail......

Be *creative* . . . HAVE FUN *!!*

You can even win two passes to the *Happiest Place on Earth* "Disneyland"
given away each Christmas just for telling us how your "Idea of the Day:"
a) improved *your* life b) improved *another's* life c) helped make the *world* a better place
(See contest details on page 369)
In the tradition of Johnny Carson's Carnac the Magnificent

Swami's Motto:

"Laugh and Be Happy and Be Here Now... *or as soon as you can!!* "

Dedication

This book is dedicated to:

My wife, Kathleen, and all my supportive family, friends
and Swami Sez Fans from around the world... Thank you

I would especially like to thank everyone in the world, including:
Norman Cousins, Sigmund Freud, Carl Jung, Carl Rogers, Edgar Cayce,
Ernest Holmes, Norman Vincent Peale, Jack Canfield, Mark Victor Hansen,
Dr. Phil, Tony Robbins, Wayne Dyer, Eckhart Tolle, Dan Brown, James Brown,
Les Brown and his Band of Renown, my "cosmic" sisters and brothers, God,
The Pope, Mort Sahl, Thoreau, Garry Treudeau, Dave Barry, Jim Carrey, Harry
Carey, Harry Potter, Henny Youngman, Lenny Bruce, Allen Ginsberg, Steve
Allen, Woody Allen, Steve Martin, George Carlin, George Jessell, George
Burns, Andy Rooney, Mickey Rooney, Rosemary Clooney, Robin Williams,
Billy Crystal, Chris Rock, Sharon Stone, Oliver Stone, Benny Hill, Napoleon
Hill, Rabbi Hillel, Dennis Miller, Mitch Miller, Dave Chappelle, Dave Attell,
Jon Stewart, Stephen Colbert, Johnathan Swift, Jonathan Winters, Richard
Pryor, Eddie Murphy, Audie Murphy, Lorne Michaels and the Saturday Night
Players, Mad Magazine, National Lampoon, Firesign Theatre, Comedy Central,
Cheech and Chong (Dave's not here!!), Dick Cavett, Tony Dow, James Taylor,
Mike Wallace, Anderson Cooper, Mark Twain, Ben Franklin, Ben and Jerry,
Oscar Wilde, F.Scott Fitzgerald, Bertrand Russell, Viktor Frankl, Deepak
Chopra, Steve Rizzo, Steve Rossi, Maxwell Maltz, Walt Whitman, Walt Disney,
Walter Knott, Wally World, Where's Waldo, The Griswalds, Imogene Coca,
Albert Einstein, Albert Brooks, Mel Brooks, Babbling Brooks, John Waters,
The Hanging Gardens of Babylon, Johnny Depp, Randy Newman, "Weird Al"
Yankovich, Al Franken, Al Gore, Gore Vidal, Aristotle, Plato, Socrates, Isaac
Bashevis Singer, Bryan Singer, Superman, Singer Brothers: Russell and Donnie
("The Donz"), my third grade teacher, Miss Loretta Anderson (who I had a big
crush on), my fifth grade teacher, "'Ol' Miss Cole" (who was real mean, but I
learned a lot, memorizing all the great poets / artists), Leonardo DaVinci,
Michelangelo, Edgar Allan Poe, Larry, Moe and Curly Joe, Moe Betta, Joe
Mama, The Mojo Brothers, Mojo Nixon, The Blues Brothers, Confucius,
Copernicus, Galileo, William James, Alvin Toffler, Abraham Maslow, Leo
Buscaglia (my teacher and mentor at USC), Art Buchwald, Buckminster Fuller,
Tesla, Voltaire, Paracelsus, Maimonides, Petrarch, Cicero, Descarte, Stan
Cartman, Trey Parker, Fess Parker, Matt Groening, Homer, Babe Ruth, Barry
Bonds, Garry Shandling, Lewis Black, Jack Black, Wolfman Jack, Wolf
Blitzer, Wolfgang Puck, Jack Benny, Bob Hope, Red Skelton, Carrot Top, Rex
Meredith, Allan Sherman, my assistant, Baba Ganoush, Og Mandino, Harry
Houdini, P.T. Barnum,The Great Merlin, Art Kunkin, Paul Krassner, Sheldon
Saltman, Lou Adler, Bill Maher, Bill Clinton, Bobby Vinton, Little Richard,
Ray Charles, Peter Max, Jamie Foxx, Redd Foxx, Harry Fox, Jeff Foxworthy,

Sunday Lox, Danny Begelman, Rob Reiner, Nik Venet, Bruce Willis, Willie Dixon, Muddy Waters, B.B. King, Don King, Alan King, Martin Luther King, Rodney King, Prince, Princess Di, Patty Duke, House of Rothschild, David Rockefeller, Bill Gates, Warren Buffett, Roger and Robert Towne, David Bowie, Trini Lopez, Steve Miller, Steve Tyler, Mick Jagger, Bro. Bruce & the Harmonica Virgins, Billy Preston, Bruce Springstein, Jerry Springer, Jerry Seinfeld, Jerry Lewis, Jerry Lee Lewis, Engelbert Humperdinck (who recorded by song, "Don't Touch That Dial" on CBS/Epic Records), Question Mark and the Mysterians (I went on tour with in the seventies: "96 Tears"), Chuck Berry, Bo Diddley, Peter Gabriel, Charley Pride, Jack Segal, Lieber and Stoller, Irving Berlin, ASCAP, NARAS (The Grammies), Grandma Moses, John Gray, Buddy Kaye, Moori Bey and Claudia Rivers, Joan Rivers, Phyllis Diller, Roseanne, Wanda Sykes, Pooty Tang ("wah dey tah, my brother!!"), Jeffrey Briar, Dr. Madan Kataria / Laughter Yoga, Church of Truth Through Humor, Association for Applied and Therapeutic Humor / Allen Klein, Gesundheit! Institute / Dr. Patch Adams, Dennis Adams, Stuart Wilde, Melody Fleming, Jon Dosa, Palm Springs Writers Guild, Dan Millman, Raymond Moody, my party planner, Mary Wahner, Whoopi, Isis, Osiris, Athena, Oprah, Tracy Ullman, Ellen Degeneres, Rita Rudner, Emile Coué, Alfred Korzybski, Edward Bernays, John Bartlett, Noah Webster, Peter Roget, Herbert Spencer, Manley P. Hall, Howard Stern, Pee Wee Herman, Tim Curry, Tim Burton, Naomi Judd, Mike Judge, Judge Judy, George Lucas, Steven Spielberg, James Dean, John Dean, Howard Dean, Jimmie Dean, Kevin Bacon, Sir Francis Bacon, Shakespeare, John Beluchi, Gilda Radnor, Mom and Dad (Dad was the comedian of the family), The Aunt Shirley Show, Jay Leno (*my comedy instructor 30 years ago*), Johnny Carson, "Carnac the Magnificent," David Letterman, Conan O'Brien, Bernie Mac, Bernie Siegel, Bill Cosby, Crosby Stills and Nash, Pat Paulsen, Smothers Brothers,Wavy Gravy, Kinky Friedman, Bill Murray, Chevy Chase, Steven S. Sadleir, Dr. Russell Christopher, Dr.Tom Costa, Robert Schuller, Marianne Williamson, Andrew Weil, Gandhi, John Candy, Amos 'n' Andy, Nostradamas, St. Germain, Lao Tzu, Krishna, Buddah, Jesus, Baba Ji, Maharishi, Ram Das, Mitch and Laurie Santell and Family, Thomas and Dr. Rhonda Clifton Lyons, John, Karen and Curt Hanlen, Jan and Frank Battaglia, Jan and Chris Kayser, Lynn and William Vaughan, Dodie and John McMurray, Judy and Ross Abbasi, Karen Orell, Judee Picone, Judy Hoyt, Cynthia Gray, Linda Ayers, Mike and Arlene Gibson, Kathleen Clark Photography, Toni Galisky, Caroline and Stephen McLean, Lena and Steven Kowalsky, Johanna and Steven Wasserman, Arlan Berglas, Pat and Bob Hughes, Bud Farley, Cameron Hall, Bro. Joseph Leavell, Phil ("The Joker") McLeod and Ruth Ann, Sharie and Dan Bohlmann, Roxy, Cher, Sharei, Gramma Bunny, Graphtek, The Akashic Records and Ron, the instructor at Pizza 4-U Great Comedians Traffic School (whose slow pace allowed me to finish this book!)

If your name is listed above and you haven't died yet: call, write, fax or e-mail and get your free autographed copy

ix

TABLE OF CONTENTS

Swami Sez
Trade the Blues
for Brownies

TOPIC
AND
AFFIRMATION
OF THE
DAY

*Listed in
Alphabetical Order*

*"A negative thought is like a ball
coming straight at you...
A positive affirmation is like the bat you use
to smack that ball right out of the park!!!"*
— Swami Sez

S W A M I   S E Z   T O P I C S

One Idea Can Change Your World

One Idea Can Change Your World

One Idea Can Change Your World

Sometimes when your life
seems to come u n f u r l e d ...
Remember, just ONE IDEA
can change your WORLD

One Idea Can Change Your World

100 Top Celebrity Birthdays

Jan	8	Elvis Presley	Aug	4	Elizabeth, The Queen Mother
Jan	15	Martin Luther King, Jr.	Aug	6	Andy Warhol
Jan	17	Benjamin Franklin	Aug	12	George Hamilton
Jan	29	Oprah Winfrey	Aug	13	Don Ho
Feb	1	Clark Gable	Aug	16	Madonna
Feb	6	Babe Ruth	Aug	17	Mae West
Feb	12	Abraham Lincoln	Aug	19	Gene Roddenberry
Feb	15	Galileo	Aug	22	Ray Bradbury
Feb	22	George Washington	Aug	27	Mother Teresa
Feb	28	Earl Scheib	Aug	28	Leo Tolstoy
Mar	2	Dr. Seuss	Aug	30	Warren Buffett
Mar	7	Dinah Shore	Aug	31	Maria Montessori
Mar	14	Einstein	Sep	1	"Dr. Phil" McGraw
Mar	24	Harry Houdini	Sep	5	Raquel Welch
Mar	28	August Anheuser Busch, Jr.	Sep	12	Ruben Studdard
Apr	2	Hans Christian Andersen	Sep	15	Prince Harry
Apr	4	Muddy Waters	Sep	16	B.B. King
Apr	10	Joseph Pulitzer	Sep	23	Ray Charles
Apr	12	David Letterman	Sep	26	Jack LaLanne
Apr	13	Thomas Jefferson	Sep	29	Jerry Lee Lewis
Apr	15	Leonardo Da Vinci	Oct	2	Groucho Marx
Apr	23	William Shakespeare	Oct	4	Alvin Toffler
Apr	28	Jay Leno	Oct	9	John Lennon
May	6	Sigmund Freud	Oct	13	Lenny Bruce
May	11	Salvador Dali	Oct	16	Noah Webster
May	12	Yogi Berra	Oct	17	Evel Knievel
May	18	Pope John Paul II	Oct	18	Chuck Berry
May	24	Bob Dylan	Oct	20	Art Buchwald
May	26	Al Jolson	Oct	21	Alfred Nobel
May	28	Dr. Patch Adams	Oct	23	Johnny Carson
May	29	John F. Kennedy	Oct	25	Pablo Picasso
May	30	Mel Blanc	Oct	28	Bill Gates
Jun	1	Marilyn Monroe	Oct	30	Ruth Gordon
Jun	8	Frank Lloyd Wright	Nov	3	Roseanne Barr
Jun	10	Judy Garland	Nov	4	Will Rogers
Jun	18	Paul McCartney	Nov	14	Prince Charles
Jun	23	Johannes Gutenberg	Nov	21	Voltaire
Jun	24	Norman Cousins	Nov	24	Dale Carnegie
Jun	28	Mel Brooks	Nov	28	Jon Stewart
Jul	4	Rube Goldberg	Nov	30	Winston Churchill
Jul	5	P.T. Barnum	Dec	5	Little Richard
Jul	6	Dalai Lama	Dec	8	Flip Wilson
Jul	8	John D. Rockefeller	Dec	9	Emmet Kelly
Jul	9	Nicola Tesla	Dec	12	Frank Sinatra
Jul	12	Buckminster Fuller	Dec	14	Nostradamus
Jul	14	Woody Guthrie	Dec	16	Arthur C. Clarke
Jul	15	Rembrandt	Dec	17	Beethoven
Jul	21	Marshall McLuhan	Dec	18	Keith Richards
Jul	26	Mick Jagger	Dec	21	Frank Zappa
Jul	30	Arnold Schwarzenneger	Dec	24	Swami Sez
Jul	31	J.K. Rowlings	Dec	25	Jesus / Carlos Castanada

One Idea Can Change Your World

Church of Truth Through Humor / Swami Sez Press

Who is
Swami Sez?

Swami Sez is...
the wisdom of the ages
and all the great sages
played upon all the world's stages
cosmically courageous
sometimes outrageous
and sometimes just plain
laugh-out-loud funny!!

And Swami Sez:

is the spiritual and humorous pen name of
Author, Entertainer, Humorist and
Voting Grammy Member
Bruce E. Singer

What is the
Church of Truth Through Humor?

Founded on the bedrock of the
Mighty "Ah! Ha!" and the Hilarious "Ha! Ha!!"
All practitioners believe a good laugh
beats three of a kind every time
And all believers know that
God is in the humor, as in
"Oh *God,* that's *funny!!!*"
Welcome now to the ever expanding
united-in-laughter congregation of the
Church of Truth Through Humor...
Laugh your ✳✳✳ off!!

<u>ABC's</u>
The Basics

S W A M I   S E Z

Awareness
Becomes
Consciousness

Today's Affirmation:

I am...
and so are you

Idea of the Day:

One Idea Can Change Your World

ABILITY
Using Your..

S W A M I   S E Z

**You are the only person on earth
who can use your ability**
(Walk your talk: less talk...more walk)

Today's Affirmation:

*I tap into my ability to explore each possibility...
I go with the good one*

Idea of the Day:

It is never too late to be
what you might have been

ABUNDANCE
Availability Of..

S W A M I S E Z

A life of abundance is all I see...
simply because I believe in
something greater in me

Today's Affirmation:

Abundance is everywhere—I see it...
I open my eyes and be it

Idea of the Day:

There is enough
of everything
for everybody

ABUNDANCE
(Have As Much As You Want!)

S W A M I   S E Z

The abundance of the universe has no favorites...
help yourself!!

Today's Affirmation:

Today I eat abundantly from the buffet table of life

Idea of the Day:

"Ideas are like rabbits —
you get a couple
and learn how to handle them...
and pretty soon you have a dozen"
— *John Steinbeck*

One Idea Can Change Your World

©2006 Church of Truth Through Humor / Swami Sez Press / B.E.Singer All Rights Reserved

ACCOMPLISHMENT
Key To..

S   W   A   M   I   S   E   Z

Time, patience and perseverance will accomplish all things

Today's Affirmation:

I am patient and persevere...
to create what I need to naturally appear

Idea of the Day:

"Between saying and doing...
many shoes are worn out"
— *Italian saying*

Cinderella Accomplishment:
The Handsome Prince
finally found his solemate

ACCOMPLISHMENT
Secret Of..

Just do it!!
*(So, if you need a new pair of sneakers...
just go down to the local sports emporium
and buy them!!)*

Today's Affirmation:

*If it is for the highest and greatest good...
I just do it*

Idea of the Day:

The way to get to the top...
is to get off your bottom

A little bit of something...
beats a lot of nothing

People may doubt what you say...
but they will believe what you do

ACCOMPLISHMENT
Shared Credit

SWAMI SEZ

If it is to be..
It is up to me
(..and thee !!)

Today's Affirmation:

I take all necessary steps to accomplish my goals

Idea of the Day:

Actions speak louder than words...
but not as often

ACHIEVEMENT
..And "Receivement"

S W A M I S E Z

What you can conceive and believe... you will achieve and receive*

Today's Affirmation:

As I believe... I receive

Idea of the Day:

Today is Elvis Presley's birthday
(January 8, 1935)
"Don't criticize what you don't understand, son...
you never walked in that man's shoes"

*Elvis' Achievement:
It is estimated that this
Grammy Award Winning Artist
has sold over
one billion records worldwide

One Idea Can Change Your World

ACHIEVEMENT
Individual..

S W A M I   S E Z

In any park, in any city...
you will *never* see a statue of a committee

T o d a y' s   A f f i r m a t i o n :

Everything is within me as a seed
to manifest and achieve... everything I need

I d e a   o f   t h e   D a y :

You can't make footprints
in the sand
by sitting down

Successful achievement is knowing that
because of you... the world is a little better

Rise to the quest...
and do your best

ACHIEVEMENT
Secret of all..

S W A M I S E Z

"Will and Grace"

Today's Affirmation:

I walk with grace... knowing everything is THY will, not MY will

Idea of the Day:

Every great achievement
was once thought
impossible or impractical

"You make zero percent
of the shots you don't take"
— *Michael Jordan*

ACTION
Taking..

S W A M I S E Z

Take your pulse
If it's still there... you've got things to do !!

Stay in action... for maximum satisfaction
("Nothing changes 'til it moves" —Einstein)

Today's Affirmation:

I wake up each morning and write a "To Do" list for the day
(I quit <u>stewin'</u> on it... and start <u>doin'</u> on it)

Idea of the Day:

Feeling listless?
Make a list

Stay in action... for maximum satisfaction

The smallest deed
is better than the
greatest intention

"Somebody has to do something...
and it's just incredibly pathetic
that it has to be us"
— Jerry Garcia
The Grateful Dead

ADVICE

..From A Trusted Source

S W A M I S E Z

Hear me now...
and thank me later!!

Today's Affirmation:

I am thankful for the insight of experts

Idea of the Day:

IT HURTS
WHEN I DO
THIS...

DON'T DO
THAT!

One Idea Can Change Your World

AGE

S W A M I   S E Z

Age doesn't matter...
unless you're cheese or wine

---✸---

Today's Affirmation:

*I realize I am ageless and that I am only as old as I feel
(age is not my cage)*

Idea of the Day:

Eventually you will
reach a point when you
stop lying about your age
and start bragging about it

AGING
Positive Side Of..

S W A M I S E Z

The older the fiddle...
the sweeter the tune

Today's Affirmation:

I am in tune with life

Idea of the Day:

"It is not the length of life... but depth of life"
— *Ralph Waldo Emerson*

One Idea Can Change Your World

AGREEABILITY
Jim Carrey Style

S W A M I   S E Z

All rightee then!!

Today's Affirmation:

I am grateful that all is right in my world
(All rightee then!!)

Idea of the Day:

Today is Martin Luther King's birthday
(January 15, 1929)
What's your dream???

ALCOHOL

Alcohol can put the "wreck" back into "recreation"
(Drink responsibly)

Today's Affirmation:

I believe in moderation in all things

Idea of the Day:

One tequila, two tequila, three tequila, floor...

ALL ABOARD

The most important ship that you board in life is called a relationship

Today's Affirmation:

As I sail through life... I honor all relationships

Idea of the Day:

Today is Benjamin Franklin's birthday
(January 17, 1706)
"There are three faithful friends —
a good wife, an old dog
and ready money"

People accept your ideas much more readily
if you tell them "Benjamin Franklin said it first"

ALONE
On Being..

Better to be alone...
than in bad company

Today's Affirmation:

I take time to be with myself...
I honor my solitude and seek only good company

Idea of the Day:

("Alone" equals "All One")

ANSWERS
Finding..

Step out within

Today's Affirmation:

The Spirit within... knows the answers to problems that confront me
(I find answers in the stillness within)

Idea of the Day:

Steps to listening to your Inner Voice:
1. Ask for inner guidance
2. Get quiet and listen
3. Trust the message
4. Act upon what you hear

One Idea Can Change Your World

ANGER
How To Handle..

If angry, count to 10 before you act...
If *really* angry, count to a thousand

Today's Affirmation:

In all situations entered...I remain calm and centered

Idea of the Day:

For every minute you are angry...
you lose 60 seconds of happiness

Tantrum Yoga will only get you
to ire consciousness

Mellow thy jello

ANSWER
The..

If you ask the question...
you're gonna' get an answer

(...if you're really listening)

Today's Affirmation:

I ask the question... and remain still until the answer comes

Idea of the Day:

If you are awake
you are in a state of
constant amazement

ANSWERS
Source Of All..

Ask somebody you know well...
ask yourself
(If it is "questionable"...it is "answerable")

Today's Affirmation:

I look to myself as a trustworthy source

Idea of the Day:

Anxiety springs from the desire
that things should happen as you wish
rather than what your higher self wills

APPRECIATION
..And Happiness

S W A M I   S E Z

Happiness comes to those
who appreciate what they already have

Today's Affirmation:

I am appreciative of all I receive...
and I am grateful for all I achieve

Idea of the Day:

Send a thank-you letter or uplifting e-mail message:
a joy for sender and receiver

APPRECIATION
..For A Job Well Done

S W A M I   S E Z

The problem with doing
something right the first time...
is nobody appreciates how difficult it was

Today's Affirmation:

I am precise... so as not to have to do it twice

Idea of the Day:

APPRECIATION
Positive..

S W A M I S E Z

You can cry because roses have thorns...
or celebrate because thorns have roses

Today's Affirmation:

I celebrate life and nature

Idea of the Day:

It's true:
You cannot experience appreciation
and a negative feeling
at the same time

ARE
Make The Best Of Wherever You..

S W A M I S E Z

Wherever you are planted...
Bloom !!

Today's Affirmation:

Right where I am is the best place I can be
I enjoy it all effortlessly...and I blossom like a flower

Idea of the Day:

ARGUING

S W A M I   S E Z

If you argue with a fool...
make sure that person is not doing the same thing

Today's Affirmation:

I am a clear communicator...
communicating clearly

Idea of the Day:

If too many people insist on arguing...
it becomes mass debating

ASKING
..A Higher Source

S W A M I S E Z

So, what would Jesus do ??
(WWJD?)

T o d a y ' s   A f f i r m a t i o n :

When I don't know...
I know I can turn to a Higher Source

I d e a   o f   t h e   D a y :

As you see the true rather than the false...
then that which is true will appear

ATTEMPTING
..Great Things

S W A M I S E Z

Better to attempt great things and blow it...
than succeed at meaningless things
and just get by

Today's Affirmation:

I enthusiastically embark on a great new adventure

Idea of the Day:

Today is Oprah Winfrey's birthday
(January 29, 1954)
"Doing the best at this moment
puts you in the best place
for the next moment"

OPRAH
THE OPRAH WINFREY SHOW

One Idea Can Change Your World

ATTITUDE
It's All About..

Make the rest of your life...
the best of your life
(Begin right now...this will prevent "hardening of the attitudes!!")

Today's Affirmation:

I have an attitude of gratitude and receptivity...
and look to the future with "positivity"

Idea of the Day:

The greatest discovery of any generation
is that human beings can
alter their life by
altering their attitude

The problem is not the problem...
the problem is your *attitude* about the problem

ATTITUDE IS EVERYTHING *!!*

Attitude determines altitude

AWARENESS

Be here NOW...
or you'll miss it

Today's Affirmation:

I am ever present

Idea of the Day:

Present moment awareness is all there is

Be aware of being aware

Solving great mysteries:
Your car keys
are right where you left them

One Idea Can Change Your World

<u>BAD</u>
When It All Seems So..

S   W   A   M   I   S   E   Z

Ask:
And what's the *good thing??*

When the negative appears... I focus my attention on the positive (and the positive appears)

Idea   of   the   Day:

Today is Clark Gable's birthday
(February 1, 1901)
Tomorrow IS another day

One Idea Can Change Your World

BAD INFLUENCES
Eliminating..

See ya...
wouldn't want to be ya
(Don't let anyone rent space inside your head)

Today's Affirmation:

I choose my friends for their exemplary character

Idea of the Day:

Today is Ground Hog Day
"The Shadow Knows..."

BEATLES
Love Those..

S W A M I S E Z

"The love you take...
is equal to the love you make"

Today's Affirmation:

When I'm down or depressed,
I put on my favorite Beatles song… and sing along

Idea of the Day:

The Beatles
with Comedians Steve Rossi and Marty Allen
1st appearance on The Ed Sullivan Show
February 9, 1964

BECOMING

On..

S W A M I   S E Z

There's nothing to become...
you already *are!!*

Today's Affirmation:

I am that I am

Idea of the Day:

One Idea Can Change Your World

<u>BED</u>
Motivation To Get Out Of...

S W A M I S E Z

The day will happen...
whether you get out of bed or not

Today's Affirmation:

*When life is challenging... I can still "**FISO**"*
(<u>F</u>unction...<u>In</u>...<u>S</u>pite...<u>Of</u>...)

Idea of the Day:

Some of the greatest minds
in Western Civilization
were manic-depressives
who learned to *"FISO"*

BEGIN
Where To..

Begin right where you are

Today's Affirmation:
I begin where I am...
and become what I give myself the power to be

Idea of the Day:

Today is Babe Ruth's birthday
(February 6, 1895)
Babe Ruth began where he was...
and became what he gave himself
the power to be
(You can, too!!)

"The beginning is half the whole...
Well begun is half done"
— Horace

BEGINNINGS
New..

Today is the first day of the rest of your life
(What happens in yesterday...
STAYS in yesterday)

Today's Affirmation:

I refuse to cringe at over-used colloquialisms

Idea of the Day:

BEING
..Yourself

You can't spray-paint the stripes off a zebra
and call it a horse...
(Be who you are)

Today's Affirmation:

I affirm my unique characteristics

Idea of the Day:

BELIEF
Eliminating The Superfluous

In the word "Belief..."
get rid of the "f"... get rid of the "lie"
and all that is left is just *"Be"*

Today's Affirmation:

*"Let it be... let it be... let it be... let it be...
There will be an answer... Let it be - eeee* – Paul McCartney / The Beatles

Idea of the Day:

Beliefs create attitudes... Attitudes create feelings
Feelings create actions... Actions create results

Warning tag on Superman costume:
"Wearing of this garment
does not enable you to fly"

One Idea Can Change Your World

BEVERAGES
...Of The Blues

S W A M I S E Z

Blues beverages:
"Muddy Water" and "Black Coffee"
(Sprite and Snapple are not)

Today's Affirmation:

I drink from the crystal clear fountain of life

Idea of the Day:

Refreshed, I enjoy my day

BLESSINGS

While others are adding up their troubles... there's you, counting your blessings

---

Today's Affirmation:

*I am too blessed to be stressed...
and too anointed to be disappointed*

Idea of the Day:

"For every one that asketh receiveth
and he that seeketh findeth
and to him that knocketh it shall be opened"
— Luke 11:10

BLESSINGS
Counting Your..

S W A M I S E Z

Count your blessings
(use both hands)

Today's Affirmation:

Though I may have issues that I must mount...
I have more blessings than I can count

Idea of the Day:

You are a blessing to yourself, to the world
and to the day in which you are now living

Today is Abraham Lincoln's birthday
(February 12, 1809)
Lincoln freed the slaves...
Refuse to be a slave to negative thinking !//

One Idea Can Change Your World

<u>BLUES</u>
Places To Have The..

Hard times in Minneapolis or Seattle is probably just clinical depression (Chicago, St. Louis and Kansas are *still* the best places to have the blues)

Today's Affirmation:
I choose the environment that gives me the most happiness...
I choose to lose the blues

Idea of the Day:

"The Blues"
is yesterday's news

After a bad storm...
look for the rainbow

BLUES
Who Can Sing The..

S W A M I S E Z

If your name is Moe, Little Joe or Big Willie...
you have the right to sing the blues
*If your name is Amber, Rainbow or Megan...
you have no right to sing the blues*

Today's Affirmation:

Today is February 14th... Happy Valentine's Day!!
Give the blues a shove — today I choose a song of love

Idea of the Day:

"What the world needs now... is love sweet love
it's the only thing that there's just too little of"
— Bert Bacharach / Hal David

BOUNCING BACK

S W A M I S E Z

Resilience
is
Brilliance

Today's Affirmation:

If I am down...
I bounce back up !!

Idea of the Day:

Today is Galileo's birthday
(February 15, 1564)
"All truths are easy to understand
once they are discovered...
the point is to discover them"

"You are a child of the Universe
no less than the trees and the stars
you have a right to be here...
and whether or not, it is clear to you
no doubt the Universe is unfolding as it should"
— *Desiderata*

BREATHING
Conscious..

S W A M I   S E Z

You'll take about 23,000 breaths today
(remember to exhale)

T o d a y ' s   A f f i r m a t i o n :
Whenever I feel blue... I start breathing again
(Each moment... I remember to breathe in life)

I d e a   o f   t h e   D a y :

Inhale *healing...*
Exhale *pain...*

When you are paying attention to your breathing...
you cannot be thinking of anything else at the same time

THINGS TO
DO TODAY
1. inhale
2. exhale
3. inhale
4. exhale
5. inhale
6. exhale
7. inhale
8. exhale
9. inhale
10. exhale
11. inhale
12. exhale
13. inhale

O n e   I d e a   C a n   C h a n g e   Y o u r   W o r l d

BREVITY

S W A M I   S E Z

"Let thy words be few"
— Ecclesiastes 5.2

Today's Affirmation:

I speak clearly... and succinctly

Idea of the Day:

Brevity is the soul of wit

One Idea Can Change Your World

BRIDGES
Burning..

Avoid burning bridges...
you'll be surprised how often
you have to cross the same river

Today's Affirmation:

*Mistreatment I reject...
I treat all people with courtesy and respect*

Idea of the Day:

One Idea Can Change Your World

BUMMER
How To Take A..

Sure, it may be a bummer...
just don't take it *personally!!*

Today's Affirmation:
I remind myself that no matter what happens...

I DO NOT TAKE IT PERSONALLY!!

Idea of the Day:

My problems are like water off a duck's back
(see page 341)

Relive the whole experience
from the 'humor perspective'

BUSY
Keeping..

S W A M I   S E Z

If you're not busy...
maybe you did it right the first time

Today's Affirmation:

It's okay to do nothing...
if there is nothing to do

Idea of the Day:

One Idea Can Change Your World

CALMING DOWN
..Musically

S W A M I S E Z

"Compose yourself, Beethoven"

Today's Affirmation:

I hum a tune...
and know my life is in harmony

Idea of the Day:

CAN DO
What You..

S W A M I S E Z

Do all you can about what you can
All the rest...just let it go

Today's Affirmation:

I do what I can...
and I am my own greatest fan

Idea of the Day:

Today is George Washington's birthday
(February 22, 1732)
"I think I might just
chop down a cherry tree today"

I Can...
If I Think
I Can!™
"Canned
Cherries"

In the future, to the question:
On what day were the Great Presidents born?
The bright student will answer..."Monday!"

One Idea Can Change Your World

CAPRICIOUSNESS

Life is just a "chowl o' berries"
(Can you say "Lake Titicaca" 3 times without smiling??)

Today's Affirmation:

Today... I remember to have fun !!

Idea of the Day :

CAREER CHOICES
Eliminating..

S W A M I   S E Z

If you don't know sh*t from shinola...
you should aspire to be
neither a plumber nor a shoe cobbler

Today's Affirmation:

The perfect career or position is mine

Idea of the Day:

CAUSE
..And Effect

S W A M I S E Z

Cause and effect is a taskmaster to the unwise... and a servant to the wise

---

Today's Affirmation:

I acknowledge that Isaac Newton is correct:
For every action… there is an equal and opposite reaction

Idea of the Day:

Cowboy wisdom:
Don't squat with spurs on

CHALLENGES

Rather than limiting your challenges...
challenge your limits

Today's Affirmation:

I accept all challenges
that are for the highest and greatest good

Idea of the Day:

You can run with the big dogs...
or sit on the porch and bark

CHANCES
Second..

SWAMISEZ

If you woke up breathing...
Congratulations *!!!*
(You have another chance)

Today's Affirmation:

*I know that every breath is another chance...
to overcome fear, doubts and "can'ts"*

Idea of the Day:

Stillness in the face of chaos
brings with it *clarity* and *insight*

You don't drown by falling in the water...
you drown by staying there

CHANGE
Welcoming..

S W A M I S E Z

If you do what you've always done... you'll be what you've always been

Today's Affirmation:

I welcome change

Idea of the Day:

Today is Earl Scheib's birthday
(February 28, 1907)
"I'll paint any car for $29.95"

One Idea Can Change Your World

CHANGE

What Can Be Better Than..

S W A M I   S E Z

Change is good...
dollars are better

Today's Affirmation:

I love to save and spend...
because money is my friend

Idea of the Day:

Change is inevitable...
except from a
vending machine

There are 293 ways to make change for a dollar

"We must be the change we wish to see"
— *Gandhi*

Change your thinking... change your life

One Idea Can Change Your World

©2006 Church of Truth Through Humor / Swami Sez Press / B.E.Singer All Rights Reserved

CHANGE
..What You Can

Since you can't change the past...
you might as well change the future

Today's Affirmation:

*When I can't change the situation...
I change my attitude*

Idea of the Day:

Are you change resistant...?
or improvement insistent !?

You can change the way you feel
by changing the way you think

To change your life...
start immediately

CHARACTER

Character is defined by what you do... when no one else is looking

I am honest and trustworthy...
regardless

Character is what you are...
Reputation is what people think you are

Today is Dr. Seuss' birthday
(March 2, 1904)
Write something
"Seussian:"

CHEERING UP

Cheer up...
life in not a "duress" rehearsal

With only faith and never fear…
I live a life of joy and cheer

Idea of the Day:

"The best way to cheer yourself up
is to try to cheer somebody else up"
— *Mark Twain*

CHOCOLATE
Color Me..

Trade the Blues
for Brownies!!

I'd trade the blues for brownies any day!!!

Chocolate contains the "feel good" chemical
Phenylethylamine
that boosts the production of serotonin...
an important mood elevating neurotransmitter

(Phenylethylamine was found to be abundantly present
in the brains of people who are in love)

MARCH 5

CHOICE

S W A M I S E Z

This...
or something better

Today's Affirmation:

*I speak my voice...
because I know I have choice*

Idea of the Day:

What a difference 30 years makes...
1976: moving to California because it's "cool"
2006: moving to California because it's warm

CHOICES
..As Clue To Character

Your choices tell you unerringly...
who you are

Today's Affirmation:

As I choose...
so I am

Idea of the Day:

Between two evils
choose neither
Between two goods
choose both

One Idea Can Change Your World

CLEANING UP
..Your Act

"Darn, heck, golly, gee-whiz!!"

Today's Affirmation:

#@!!!!#@!!!*!*
Didn't that feel good??

Idea of the Day:

Today is Dinah Shore's birthday
(March 7, 1917)
Dinah Shore earned lots of money
representing cheery optimism
and southern charm...
(Try it and see what happens:
For the next 30 days, be cheery, charming and optimistic)

CLEAR THINKING

Be clear and ask for what you want...
'cause it's coming
(...fast!!)

Today's Affirmation:

As I knock...
I know the door opens

Idea of the Day:

Every day is another chance
for you to decide
how you want it to be

COME BACK
Making A..

S W A M I S E Z

It's hard to make a comeback... when you haven't been anywhere

---

Today's Affirmation:

I boldly venture forth...
No fear

Idea of the Day:

COMMUNICATING
..For Maximum Effect

Speak clear as a bell...
and your words will ring true
(Magician that you are: your word is your wand!!)

Today's Affirmation:

The words I seek...
are the truth I speak

Idea of the Day:

Know what you want to say...
Say it in a convincing way

Clear Communication:
American Airlines Peanut Pack Instructions
"Open packet, eat peanuts"

"The most important thing in communications
is to hear what isn't being said"
— *Peter Drucker*

COMPLAINTS
Timing Of..

S W A M I   S E Z

No whine...before it's time
(shoulda'... woulda'... coulda'...
you didn't... get over it... move on)

Today's Affirmation:

*I am grateful and positive...
that I am positively grateful*

Idea of the Day:

COMPLETIONS

Never put off 'til tomorrow...
what you can avoid all together

Today's Affirmation:
I do what needs to be done...
then I set aside time to have some fun

Idea of the Day:

You can't dig half a hole

COMPLIMENTS
Sincere..

S W A M I   S E Z

Be sincere with your compliments...
most people can tell the difference between
sugar and saccharine

Today's Affirmation:

I am genuine and sincere

Idea of the Day:

COMPULSING
One Word Cure For..

S W A M I S E Z

NEXT!!

Today's Affirmation:

Yesterday's gone...
Today I move on

Idea of the Day:

Today is Einstein's Birthday
(March 14, 1879)
Think of something smart *!!*

One Idea Can Change Your World

74

CONSCIENCE

Conscience is what hurts...
when everything else feels so good

Today's Affirmation:

I trust my higher conscience
to guide my every action

Idea of the Day:

"Be the master of your will
and the slave of your conscience"
— *Yiddish saying*

CONSCIOUSNESS
Achieving Higher..

S W A M I S E Z

Move into a significantly higher altitude...
and breathe a lighter air

Today's Affirmation:

I have no fear because higher consciousness is here
As I breathe the lighter air... I eliminate every care

Idea of the Day:

Become conscious of being conscious

One alone in consciousness is a majority

Awakened consciousness will align you with your life purpose

Allow consciousness to emerge through
whatever you do

"This above all...
To thine own self be true"
— *Shakespeare*
Hamlet

CONVERSATIONS

S W A M I S E Z

It's all right to hold a conversation...
but let go of it now and then !!
(Make sure your train of thought has a caboose)

Today's Affirmation:

*In conversations, I share the floor...
so that all can have a space to speak out more*

Idea of the Day:

Since you have two ears and one mouth...
listen twice as much as you speak

Today is St. Patrick's Day
May the luck of the Irish be yours today

 St. Patrick was Patron Saint of Ireland
He is said to have given
a sermon from a hill top
that drove all the snakes from Ireland
(Of note, no snakes were ever native to Ireland)
But it's a good opportunity to party...
Green beer for all my friends !!!

COUNT
Making Every Moment..

There is no room for inanity...
if you want to keep your sanity

Today's Affirmation:

*I choose to speak and spend my day...
with those who truly have something to say*

Idea of the Day:

COURAGE

Courage is fear
that has said its prayers

("Those who stand for nothing...fall for anything")
—Alexander Hamilton

Today's Affirmation:

I fear nothing or no one...
I AM FREE !!

Idea of the Day:

"Courage is grace under pressure"
— *Ernest Hemingway*

<u>COURSE</u>
..Correction

S W A M I   S E Z

If you don't change the course you're on...
you will end up where you're headed
(except a Nietzsche Existential Map, which would have
"You Are Here" written everywhere)

Today's Affirmation:
I choose my direction, I choose my slate...
because I am the master of my own fate

Idea of the Day:

"God is dead," signed Nietzsche
("Nietzsche is dead," signed God)

Today is the first day of Spring
(Vernal Equinox)

"Spring is nature's way to say... Let's party *!!!*"
— *Robin Williams*

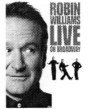

One Idea Can Change Your World

CRAZY?
Am I..

If you do the same thing
and expect a different result...then, yes
(Being a little crazy... can keep you from going insane)

Today's Affirmation:

Today I "cut loose" a little bit...
just for the fun of it!!

Idea of the Day:

When you become aware that you are crazy...
you are no longer crazy

Have you ever stood in a long line at the bank
and all of a sudden got the urge to grab
the bank's customer courtesy pen
and rip it off its beady little chain...??
You're normal !!

CRITICISM
Dealing With..

If it doesn't apply...
"let it fly"

Today's Affirmation:

Whether I receive criticism or flatter...
I let go of all that doesn't matter

Idea of the Day:

Compete with no one...
for you are forever yourself

For any bit of criticism you may raise...
sandwich between two layers of praise

CVRES
Sensual..

Better erotic...
than neurotic

Today's Affirmation:

I appreciate my body...
and the beauty of the human form

Idea of the Day:

The best cure for hypochondria
is to forget about your own body
and get involved in someone else's //

CYCLES

Sometimes sunshine, sometimes fog...
Sometimes master, sometimes dog
*(Sometimes windshield, sometimes bug,
Sometimes rebuff, sometimes hug)*

Today's Affirmation:

*Whether I feel elation or I feel strife...
I am aware and accept the cycles of life*

Idea of the Day:

Today is Harry Houdini's birthday
(March 24, 1874)
Escape the negative and
experience something
positively magical!!

CYCLES
Life..

What goes up must come down...
(So get down and get back up)

Today's Affirmation:

*I appreciate my life and all I've found...
I know what goes around comes around*

Idea of the Day:

You can not control the cycles of life...
but you can ride them like a bucking bronco or a flowing tide

*You can buy a chocolate Easter Bunny
for 75% off --- the day after Easter...
Your understanding of life cycles and business cycles
can make you wealthy
(or at least get you good prices on chocolate)*

DATING
..Advice

S W A M I S E Z

If someone says you are too good for him or her... believe them

Today's Affirmation:

*I weigh the insights of my friends' visions...
to help guide my life's decisions*

Idea of the Day:

DAY
Appreciating Each..

S W A M I S E Z

Every calendar's days
are numbered

Today's Affirmation:

In each and every way...
I appreciate each and every day

Idea of the Day:

Follow your bliss... Relish each kiss

DAY
As A Gift..

S   W   A   M   I   S   E   Z

Every day is a gift...
(even if it sucks)
("One brand new day...sign right here, please!")

T o ∂ a y ' s   A f f i r m a t i o n :

I appreciate each day...
for the gift of the lesson that comes my way

I d e a   o f   t h e   D a y :

Today is August Anheiser Busch, Jr.'s birthday
(March 28, 1899)
Everybody's got to believe in something
and I believe I'll have another beer!

DAY
Celebrating The..

Celebrate the bad days...
the good ones take care of themselves

(You can GO through another day...
or you can GROW through another day)

Today's Affirmation:

I celebrate each day ...
in work and in play!!

Idea of the Day:

Have a
"Zip-a-dee-doo-dah
Zip-a-dee-ay
Everything's going my way"
kind of day *!!*

DAY
Last..

Blues singer's epitaph...
"I *didn't* wake up this morning..."

Today's Affirmation:

Why sing the blues...
when I can chew on a big delicious brownie ??

Idea of the Day:

Everyone will be remembered...
How do you want your story to go ??

DAY
Making Your..

S W A M I S E Z

"Go ahead...
MAKE MY DAY"
— *Clint Eastwood*
"Dirty Harry"

T o d a y ' s   A f f i r m a t i o n :

I make my day...
the way I say...

I d e a   o f   t h e   D a y :

Seize The Day

One Idea Can Change Your World

DAY
Recognizing A Good..

S W A M I S E Z

You know it's a good day when you
walk into a supermarket and find a shopping cart
with all the wheels going in the same direction

Today's Affirmation:

I find appreciation in the smallest of miracles

Idea of the Day:

Remember, a day without sunshine
is like... well,
night!

DAY
Shaping Your..

S W A M I   S E Z

Today stretches ahead of me
waiting to be shaped... and I am the sculptor

Today's Affirmation:

I shape my body by what I eat and do...
I shape my thoughts by what I believe to be true

Idea of the Day:

Today is Hans Christian Anderson's birthday
(April 2, 1805)
Stretch your creative imagination
to the most "far out place" you can take it

DAYS
Counting The..

Why count the days...
when you can make the days count!!

Today's Affirmation:

I make each day count

Idea of the Day:

Loving your days:
How do I love thee ??
Let me count the ways

©2006 Church of Truth Through Humor / Swami Sez Press / B.E.Singer All Rights Reserved

DAYS
Good..

If you don't think every day is a good one...
just try missing one!

Today's Affirmation:

I realize with grace...
that each day has its own rhythm and pace

Idea of the Day:

Birds are chirping, flowers bloom, little children play...
sounds like it's gonna' be a magnificent day

Today is Muddy Waters' birthday
(April 4, 1915)
Muddy was one of the Fathers of the Blues…
Why not celebrate with a big chewy brownie and a glass of milk?

(see Swami Sez Brownie Recipe on page 368)

DECISIONS

Indecision...
is a decision

Today's Affirmation:

In life, I enjoy the ride...
when it comes to decisions — I decide!

Idea of the Day:

"Problems come when the individual
tries to hand over the decision making
to a committee"
— *Rupert Murdoch*

There are no wrong decisions
(only different lessons)

DECREE
..For Self-Improvement

S   W   A   M   I   S   E   Z

"Every day... in every way
I am getting better and better"
*(Famed Autosuggestion Founder, Dr. Emile Coué advised his patients to repeat
this affirmation 15-20 times a day for 30 days — Try it: you'll see results !!)*

Today's Affirmation:

The following affirmation, I learn to the letter:
"Every day in every way...I am getting better and better"

Idea   of   the   Day:

Replace in your mind any negative taunt...
and affirm right now for what you want

One Idea Can Change Your World

DEEP DEPRESSION
What To Do About..

Snap out of it... Get over it
"Fuhgedaboudit"
Turn it over to the "Big Guy driving the bus"

Today's Affirmation:

I let go... and turn it over to a Higher Power
(it can be just that simple)

Idea of the Day:

If you want to "overcome" depression, every day, bring a real joy to someone else...
Noble deeds along with hot baths can be most beneficial for lifting the spirits:
"I breathe deeply and connected...and I accelerate my cells to create the reality I prefer...
I affirm the positive and choose wellness and happiness"
(see page 317)

DEJA VU
Have You Ever Had..

S   W   A   M   I   S   E   Z

Have you ever had déjà vu?

Today's Affirmation:

Sometimes I feel that I have been here before...
(and then before that)

Idea of the Day:

Feeling like you have been in Japan before:
Asia Vu
Feeling like you've read that book before:
Page a Vu
Continually going with bland colors:
Beige a Vu
Feeling like you acted in the same play before:
Stage a Vu
Feeling like a mystic from a former lifetime:
Sage a Vu
Feeling like you've used the same condiment before
Dijon Vu

(If you think of another one...
e-mail and let Swami know)

DEPRESSED
What It's Like To Be..

S W A M I   S E Z

That's when someone says
"Have a nice day..."
and you tell them you have other plans

---※---

Today's Affirmation:

*I look for the best and most positive way...
in each and every day*

Idea of the Day:

Whatever it is...
relive the entire past experience
from a humorous perspective —
You have the power to
re-write, re-direct and edit
your tragedy into a comedy

Better to cure... than endure

Note: Natural lithium salts have done wonders
for many who have suffered from feelings of depression

If you're feeling "down with the blues"
many people have felt much better after eating a banana
This is because bananas contain tryptophan
a protein the body converts to serotonin
known to make you relax, improve your mood
and generally make you feel happy
(maybe *that* is why *monkeys* are so *happy!!*)

One Idea Can Change Your World

DEPRESSION
"Deep Knee Bends Cure.."

S   W   A   M   I   S   E   Z

Get down...
and get back up

T o d a y ' s   A f f i r m a t i o n :
When the day seems to give me "squat"
good food and exercise is what I've got...
(a n d   d e s p a i r   g i v e s   w a y   t o   j o y)
I d e a   o f   t h e   D a y :

Manic Depressive:
Easy glum, easy glow

If this book had existed in the 1930's...
there would have been no
"Great Depression"

Today is Joseph Pulitzer's birthday
(April 10, 1847)
"Screw this depression…
I'm gonna' go win me the Pulitzer Prize"
(or whatever you want)

What your mind can conceive and believe
your mind can receive and achieve

One Idea Can Change Your World

DESTINY

The future is coming...
but only you can decide where it is going

Today's Affirmation:

I welcome the future...
knowing I influence its outcome

Idea of the Day:

Follow your soul's path
Fulfill your destiny...
and transform your life

DIET
Successful..

S W A M I   S E Z

Triumph of "mind over platter"
(Diet is wishful shrinking...taste makes waist)

Today's Affirmation:

*I eat healthy and in moderation...
and remember to take my dose of Vitamin H (humor!!)*

Idea of the Day:

Eat conscious vegetables:
"I am that I yam"

Today is David Letterman's birthday
(April 12, 1947)
"I'm just trying to make a smudge
on the collective unconscious"

LAUGH YOURSELF THIN:
Researchers at Vanderbilt University discovered that 15 minutes of laughter can burn as many as 50 calories
Over the course of one year, a good laugh could burn two to four pounds of fat
even without changing your dietary habits *!!*

One Idea Can Change Your World

DIETING
Eat Yourself Thin!

True fact...
Eating celery burns more calories
than the celery contains

Today's Affirmation:

"I'm strong to the 'finich'... 'cuz I eats me spinich"
— *Popeye the Sailor Man*

Idea of the Day:

Today is Thomas Jefferson's birthday
(April 13, 1743)
Principal author of the Declaration of Independence
Celebrate the spirit of Jefferson's quill pen and be inspired to write
something profound (or real funny) right here and right now…
Okay ready, set...

"The pen is mightier than the sword...
and considerably easier to write with"
— *Marty Feldman*

DISTRACTION

S   W   A   M   I   S   E   Z

Hey...
Look over
There !!

T o d a y ' s   A f f i r m a t i o n :

I am centered and focused

I d e a   o f   t h e   D a y :

Why is it that when you are driving and looking for an address...
you turn down the radio?

<u>DO</u>
What To..

Find the thing that makes you
"come alive..."
and go do it!!

Today's Affirmation:
*I do what I love which makes me thrive...
and allows my spirit to "come alive"*

Idea of the Day:

Today is Leonardo Da Vinci's birthday
(April 15, 1452)
Each day is a blank canvas...
Create a masterpiece with your
creative imagination

![The Da Vinci Code book cover]

Doctor
Doctor's..

S W A M I   S E Z

You are in the position
to be your spirit's own physician

Today's Affirmation:

I know the doctor is in... and within
and I experience the feeling of "hee—hee—hee healing"

Idea of the Day:

"The best doctors
in the world are:
Dr. Diet, Dr. Quiet
and Dr. Merryman"
— *Jonathan Swift*

*"Hi, you're
new on
this staff,
aren't you?"*

DOCTOR'S ADVICE
Improving On..

S W A M I S E Z

You've got a heart murmur and be careful...?
I thought you said
"Get a 'hot mama' and be cheerful!!"

Today's Affirmation:

I always listen carefully

Idea of the Day:

Don't forget your Vitamin Be One

Get deep rest
(not depressed)

"The art of medicine
consists of amusing the patient
while nature cures the disease"
— Voltaire

DOING IT
Just..

Sometimes it's just easier to ask forgiveness than to ask permission

Today's Affirmation:

*If it's for my highest and greatest good...
I just do it*

Idea of the Day:

There are two reasons for doing something:
1. a really good reason
2. the *real reason*

Whatever I am ready for... is ready for me

"Each of you, regardless of position, status,
circumstances or physical condition,
is in control of your own experience"
—Seth

DONATION
The Value Of..

For a sense of clarity...donate some time to charity
*(As my cup runs over, I share my blessings
with all whom I meet)*

Today's Affirmation:

*I realize that serving others through action...
offers one of life's greatest satisfaction*

Idea of the Day:

"Make all you can
Save all you can
Give all you can"
— John Wesley

DOROTHY
Wisdom Of..

SWAMI SEZ

Appreciate where you live

Today's Affirmation:

*"There's no place like home...
there's no place like home"*

Idea of the Day:

Dorothy in the computer age:
There's no place like
http://www.home.com

Kansas Yoga:
"There's no place like Om"

DREAMING
..In Color

S W A M I S E Z

Dreaming in color...
is a pigment of your imagination

Today's Affirmation:

I know that this is a dream... and I am dreaming

Idea of the Day:

"If you can dream it... you can do it"
— *Walt Disney*

©2006 Church of Truth Through Humor / Swami Sez Press / B.E.Singer All Rights Reserved

DREAMS

Never laugh at anyone's dreams
(unless they're really funny!!)

Today's Affirmation:
I follow my dreams...
(and I appreciate my sense of humor)

Idea of the Day:

Act upon your dreams and you will find
that you have left all doubts behind

DWELLING

We attract what we dwell on...
and what we dwell on, we become
(Change your thoughts... change your life)

Today's Affirmation:

*I accentuate the positive...
and eliminate the negative*

Idea of the Day:

Today is William Shakespeare's birthday
(April 23, 1564)
Either write a play
or go out and play...
Life is too valuable to be
aimlessly moping around

<u>EARNINGS</u>
Rhyming Your Way To Greater..

Yearn,
Learn, Discern...
Earn *!!*

Today's Affirmation:

I deserve excellent wages for my
excellent talents and services

Idea of the Day:

One Idea Can Change Your World

EGO
Feeding The..

At the feast of the ego...
everyone leaves hungry

Today's Affirmation:

I subdue the ego and do my part...
to speak positively from my heart

Idea of the Day:

Egotism is the act
of seeing in yourself
what others cannot see

One nice thing about egotists:
They don't talk about other people

E-MAIL

Reach out
and
type somebody

Today's Affirmation:

I e-mail people I care about...
with something I can share about

Idea of the Day:

ENCOURAGEMENT

S W A M I   S E Z

A word of encouragement during a failure...
is worth more than a whole book of praise
after a success

Today's Affirmation:

*I appreciate and encourage
my own and others' success*

Idea of the Day:

ENLIGHTENMENT
Fast-track..

S W A M I   S E Z

Zen Crafters:
Total Enlightenment in about an hour

Today's Affirmation:

For deeper answers when I am feeling strife…
I tap into the spiritual aspect of life

Idea of the Day:

Today is Jay Leno's birthday
(April 28, 1950)
"You can not be mad
at someone who
makes you laugh --
it's as simple as that"

May you be struck by enlightening
during a brainstorm

One Idea Can Change Your World

EVERYTHING
Source Of..

SWAMI SEZ

Everything comes from within... so why go without?

Today's Affirmation:

*Act as if it IS so...
and it WILL be so*

Idea of the Day:

You can't have everything...
where would you put it?

Enlightenment comes from that blissful
empty moment of "nothingness..."
Nothing is everything

One Idea Can Change Your World

EVOLUTION
Constant..

S W A M I   S E Z

You are not the same person you were a minute ago

Today's Affirmation:

I am a product of constant change

Idea of the Day:

EXAGGERATING

S W A M I   S E Z

Don't make a mountain out of a mole-hill...
unless you have a large John Deere tractor

(For all trivia buffs: the John Deere Company was established in 1837)

Today's Affirmation:

*I remember to communicate clearly...
without exaggeration*

Idea of the Day:

EXCELLENCE
..In All Things

Whatever you do...
do it true

Today's Affirmation:

I strive for excellence

Idea of the Day:

"An idea can turn to dust or magic...
depending on the talent that rubs up against it"
— *Bill Bernbach*

EXCELLING

When you have a true desire to excel... excelling is no longer a struggle
(Those who want to succeed will find a way... those who don't will find an excuse)

Today's Affirmation:
I accept success
as the natural outcome of my efforts

Idea of the Day:

A little spark kindles a great fire

"We are what we repeatedly do...
Excellence therefore is not an act but a habit"
— *Aristotle*

MAY 4

EXEMPLARINESS

S   W   A   M   I   S   E   Z

If you can't be a good example...
at least be a horrible warning!!

Today's Affirmation:

For myself and others I set a good example...
as I strive to be the best of the representative sample

Idea of the Day:

EXPERIENCE
Learning From..

S W A M I S E Z

Experience teaches best...
because it gives you individual instruction
("Been there — done that — bought the T-shirt")

Today's Affirmation:
I learn from my experiences, whether pain or pleasure...
Each experience is a hidden treasure

Idea of the Day:

The lessons of experience are always positive...
even if the experience is not

Out of everything bad comes something good

"We all have to go through the tumbler a few times
before we can turn into a crystal"
— Elisabeth Kübler Ross

FAILS
When All Else..

S W A M I S E Z

Laugh
about it !!

T o d a y ' s   A f f i r m a t i o n :

Today, I live, love and laugh

I d e a   o f   t h e   D a y :

Today is Sigmund Freud's birthday
(May 6, 1856)
Invite your Id, Ego and Super Ego to celebrate..
How about a big chocolate brownie ??

Oedipus, shmedipus...
as long as you love your mother

One Idea Can Change Your World

FAITH

S W A M I   S E Z

Keep the faith...
then pass it on to someone else
(by holding on to nothing...you can have everything!!)

Today's Affirmation:

In perfect trust, in abiding faith, and with complete peace...
I let go of the problem and the problem does cease

Idea of the Day:

Love and fear
cannot be experienced at the same time
(because fear is the opposite of love)

"Faith is the evidence of things not seen"
— *Hebrews 11:1*

Let go of *fear...**
and grin from ear to ear
with faith in a life of joy and cheer

* What is Fear?
F= false, E= evidence, A = appearing, R= real

One Idea Can Change Your World

FEELINGS
..Of Hopelessness And Constipation

S W A M I S E Z

"This too
shall pass"

Today's Affirmation:

I know nothing is permanent, no issue too mass...
whatever problem I face, I know that "this too shall pass"

Idea of the Day:

I let go of fear and doubt
and experience peace... inner and out

FINDING
..What You Need

S W A M I S E Z

What you are looking for...
is looking for you

Today's Affirmation:

I know what I am looking for...
is already there

Idea of the Day:

FOCUS
Law of..

S W A M I   S E Z

If you focus on what you do not want...
you will get more of it

Today's Affirmation:
*I focus on what I want to create...
and I receive that on which I concentrate*

Idea of the Day:

Consider the postage stamp:
It secures success to reach its destination
by its ability to stick to one thing

Where your focus goes...
your energy flows

Stay focused:
Avoid becoming a Meanderthal

One Idea Can Change Your World

MAY 11

FOLLOW
What To..

S W A M I S E Z

Follow
your bliss
(Your opinion of me... is none of my business)

I can not miss...
if I follow my bliss

Idea of the Day:

Happily ever after... happens one day at a time

Today is Salvador Dali's birthday
(May 11, 1904)
"At the age of six, I wanted to be a cook
At seven, I wanted to be Napoleon...
and my ambition has been
growing steadily ever since"

One Idea Can Change Your World

FOOLISHNESS

S W A M I   S E Z

Talk sense to a fool...
and he'll call you foolish
(A fool and his money are soon partying)

---❋---

Today's Affirmation:

I choose to talk sense
with sensible people

Idea of the Day:

"Wise men don't need advice... fools don't take it"
— *Benjamin Franklin*

Today is Yogi Berra's birthday
(May 12, 1925)
"When you come to a fork in the road…
take it"

One Idea Can Change Your World

FORWARD
Looking..

S W A M I S E Z

Look forward...
looking back causes you to
bump into people not going your way

Today's Affirmation:

Today I make the decision... to look forward with clear vision

Idea of the day:

On a clear day... you can see forever

FREEDOM

"Freedom's just another word for nothing left to lose..."
(except maybe your Janis Joplin record collection)

Today's Affirmation:

I release my burden... I surrender my past:
"Free at last… Free at last…. Thank God Almighty, I am free at last!!"

Idea of the Day:

All is forgiven... you are free

I AM FREE

Freedom comes in being who you are
(you don't have to be who you are not)

You are free to discover
and create your own
individual path to freedom

FREUDIAN SLIP

S W A M I   S E Z

When you say one thing...
but mean your mother
(see page 127)

Today's Affirmation:
I give thanks to my parents for my life..
I forgive any of their shortcomings
(and I say to them now: "I love you, Mom and Dad")
Idea of the Day:

Forgive and live
(happily)

"If my Mamehlushin was a Tateh
(if my MOTHER was a FATHER)
things would be quite different"
— *Old Yiddish saying*

If this isn't making sense...
listen to a Pink Freud album

FRIENDLINESS

S W A M I   S E Z

Remember, it's not, "How high are you...?"
It's "Hi, how are you?"
(To have a friend, be a friend:
Friends are like icing on the cake of life)

Today's Affirmation:

Today, I will be friendly
to every person I meet

Idea of the Day:

People do not make friends...
they recognize them

Friendliness:
flowers in life's garden

One Idea Can Change Your World

FRIENDS
Making..

Make friends with yourself...
and you'll never be alone

Today's Affirmation:

I am...
my own best friend

Idea of the Day:

A friend is a gift you give yourself

By being a friend to yourself...
others will be so, too

Two's company... three's the Muskateers

One Idea Can Change Your World

FRIENDSHIP

A friend is never farther away
than needing them can reach
(Friendship is the bacon bits... in the salad of life)

Today's Affirmation:

*Indeed, I know a friend in need...
is a friend in deed (indeed!)*

Idea of the Day:

"There is a magnet in your heart
that will attract true friends
That magnet is unselfishness...
thinking of others first
When you learn to live for others
they will live for you
— *Paramahansa Yogananda*

Today is Pope John Paul II's birthday
(May 18, 1920)
What a friend we have in Jesus

FUN

All for FUN...
and
FUN for all !!

Today's Affirmation:

Today, my life is about fun

Idea of the Day:

Life is
FUNdamentally
Fun *!!*

Some fun things to do in an elevator:
1. Meow occasionally
2. Light up all the buttons
3. Say "ding" at each floor

FUTURE
Getting To The...

You won't get to the future
if your past is present
(The future is always closer than it appears to be:
It is what you make it... so make it a good one)

Today's Affirmation:

I live in the ever present moment

Idea of the Day:

"I never think of the future...
it comes soon enough"
— *Albert Einstein*

Swami Tip:
To travel to the future... just think ahead

"Very funny Scotty...
Now beam me down my clothes"

One Idea Can Change Your World

FUTURE
Your..

S W A M I   S E Z

The future's so bright...
you gotta' wear shades

Today's Affirmation:

I see a bright future...
and a bright future it will be

Idea of the Day:

Practice random acts of intelligence
and senseless acts of self control

"The future belongs to those
who believe in the beauty of their dreams"
— *Eleanor Roosevelt*

GARDENS

S W A M I   S E Z

In your garden of life...
be sure to have "thyme for yourself"
and "thyme for each other"

Today's Affirmation:

Wherever I go...
I reap what I sow

Idea of the Day:

(Explore the wonders of herbs:
"Holy Basil" is known to uplift, calm, balance and elevate spirits...
"Ginkgo Biloba" is known to enhance memory and mental clarity)

The end of the garden is at the end of the hose

Good thoughts bear good fruits
Bad thoughts bear bad fruits...
and man is his own gardener

GENIUS
..Versus Mediocrity

S W A M I   S E Z

Mediocrity is self-inflicted...
Genius is self-bestowed

There is a genius sleeping in everyone...
(and every day the sleep gets deeper)

T o d a y ' s   A f f i r m a t i o n :

I wake up to see...
the genius that is me

I d e a   o f   t h e   D a y :

"Genius is one percent inspiration
and ninety nine percent perspiration"
— *Thomas Edison*

"(Time to start sweatin')"
— *Swami Sez*

GETTING AWAY

If you're thinking about taking off somewhere...
remember, most blues transportation is a
greyhound bus or a southbound train

Today's Affirmation:

As I travel through life in its cyclical flow...
I choose where and how I want to go

Idea of the Day:

Today is Bob Dylan's birthday
(May 24, 1921)
"You don't need a weatherman
to know which way the wind blows"

Trust your instincts!

One Idea Can Change Your World

GETTING IT

Nudge... Nudge
(Wink....Wink)*!!!*
(When you finally "get it"... pass it on to someone else)

T o d a y ' s   A f f i r m a t i o n :

I get it!!

I d e a   o f   t h e   D a y :

The most important gift you could ever give yourself...
is to be who you are

"Normal is just a setting on a washing machine"
— Whoopi Goldberg

GIFTS
Ultimate..

S W A M I S E Z

The best gift for someone close...
is something that you can use yourself

Today's Affirmation:

I choose my gifts consciously

Idea of the Day:

Acknowledge your unique gifts and talents

Today is Al Jolson's birthday
(May 26, 1886)
"I'm sittin' on top of the world...
Glory Hallelujah *!!*
Don't want any millions
I'm getting my share
I've only got one suit
that's all I can wear"

One Idea Can Change Your World

GIFT
You Are The..

Be Present

Today's Affirmation:

I appreciate the gift of today...
and I am fully present

Idea of the Day:

One of the greatest gifts of healing
is the act of forgiveness:
"As you forgive... so shall you be forgiven"

One Idea Can Change Your World

MAY 28

<u>GIVING</u>

Give 'til it feels good
("Freely I give... Freely I receive")

Today's Affirmation:

Charity comes from the heart...
there's no better time than now to start

Idea of the Day:

Today is Dr. Patch Adams' birthday
(May 28, 1945)
Proponent of the medical value of laughter,
Dr. Patch Adams founded the
Gesundheit! Institute in West Virginia

Robin Williams portrayed Dr. Patch Adams in the motion picture
about Patch's life and this power of healing through laughter

Two major "Laughter Doctors" meet:
Dr. Madan Kataria, (Founder of the "Laughter Yoga Clubs Movement")
with Dr. Patch Adams

One Idea Can Change Your World

GOALS

Rhyming Your Way To Success

S W A M I   S E Z

Be consistent and persistent...
insistent and resistant

Today's Affirmation:

*I dig my way out of any hole...
and I attain my goal*

Idea of the Day:

Today is John F. Kennedy's birthday
(May 29, 1917)
The Kennedy family motto:
"A Kennedy never comes in second place"
Let the Kennedy Spirit rub off on you
(Bill Clinton shook JFK's hand ...
and he grew up to be President, too)
*Find somebody great
and go shake their hand*

*Your author
who shook Walt Disney's hand in 1955
at the Grand Opening of Disneyland
thinks that the whole world
is an amusement park*

One Idea Can Change Your World

GOALS
Setting..

S   W   A   M   I   S   E   Z

In life, whatever your goal... keep your eyes on the donut and not on the hole

---

Today's Affirmation:

I choose where I am going... so I can get there fully knowing

Idea of the Day:

Be sure to write down your goals:
Goals not written
are just wishes

Today is Mel Blanc's birthday
(May 30, 1908)
"Eh, what's up, Doc?"

Ironically, Mel Blanc
(the voice of Bugs Bunny)
was allergic to carrots

GOD
Letting Go, Letting..

S W A M I   S E Z

God's gonna' be up all night anyway...
just let Him deal with it!!
(Atheists* & Agnostics...guess you'll have to deal with it all by yourself)

Today's Affirmation:

Whatever it is in my darkest hour...
I turn it over to a Higher Power

Idea of the Day:

Prayer is when you talk to God...
Meditation is when you listen to God

"The greatest prayer you could ever pray
would be to laugh every day...
For when you do, it elevates the vibratory frequency within your being
such that you could heal your entire body"
— Ramtha

It is your God-given right to be an atheist

One Idea Can Change Your World

GOLDEN RULE
Revisited

S W A M I   S E Z

Do unto others...
as you would have them do unto you
(Sadists and Masochists, please ignore)

T o d a y ' s   A f f i r m a t i o n :

I live my life
by the Golden Rule

I d e a   o f   t h e   D a y :

Today is Marilyn Monroe's birthday
(June 1, 1926)
Take the day and be playful
"Happy Birthday,
Mist-tah' Pwez-i-dent..."

One Idea Can Change Your World

GOOD
Going For The..

S W A M I   S E Z

Take the Good...
wherever you find it
(All good things come to... a new beginning)

Today's Affirmation:

*I look only for the good...
in everything*

Idea of the Day:

All good is now mine

"If you affirm the positive
the negatives will drop off by themselves"
— *Ramana Maharshi*

GOOD
What's..

Ain't nothing like...
good poonannie
(poonannie is slang for pecan pie)

Today's Affirmation:

I appreciate everything

Idea of the Day:

GOOD DAY
Key To A..

S W A M I S E Z

Every day can be a good day
they all start out that way...
How your day *ends...depends* on what you put in it

Today's Affirmation:

I fill my day with good...
which by design, makes it a "good day"

Idea of the Day:

I love my Higher Power
and my Higher Power loves me —
WE ARE ONE

GOOD DAY
Knowing If You're Having A..

S W A M I S E Z

If you can't think of anything to complain about...
you must be having a good day

Today's Affirmation:

I choose to have a good day and all is fine...
all that is good is now mine

Idea of the Day:

"Doing good to others is not a duty
it is a joy...
for it increases your own health and happiness"
— *Zoroastor*

One Idea Can Change Your World

GRATITUDE

You can't be grateful
and unhappy at the same time
(Expect nothing... be grateful for everything)

Today's Affirmation:

*Today I demonstrate that the attitude of gratitude...
is more than a great platitude*

Idea of the Day:

GRATITUDE
..After A Big Loss

S W A M I   S E Z

Look at what you have left...
rather than what you have lost

Today's Affirmation:

Even in an unfortunate turn of the tide...
I look on the positive side

Idea of the Day:

"Whatever calamity happens to you
if you thank and praise God for it...
you turn it into a blessing"
— *William Law*

One Idea Can Change Your World

GRATITUDE
Attitude Of..

I can complain that the weather is rainy...
or I can be thankful that the grass
is getting watered for free

———————————✳———————————

Today's Affirmation:

Hail, sleet, rain or snow...
I let go... and go with the flow

Idea of the Day:

Today is Frank Lloyd Wright's birthday
(June 8, 1867)
Be the architect of your own life

GRATITUDE
Elvis Style..

"Thank you...
thank you very much!!"

I am grateful for popular music icons…
and their great music

Idea of the Day:

Thanks to Elvis *!!*
(see Page 8)

GRATITUDE

Giving Credit Where Credit Is Due

I cried because I had no shoes...
until I met a man who had no problem
increasing my Master Card limit

Today's Affirmation:

*I give credit...
where credit is due*

Idea of the Day:

Today is Judy Garland's birthday
(June 10, 1922)
Go to the mall today
and buy a pair of
red shoes

JUNE 11

GRATITUDE
..In Spite Of It All

S W A M I   S E Z

"Nice to be here...
Nice to be anywhere"
— Keith Richards
The Rolling Stones

Today's Affirmation:

*I am in appreciation
of the most basic of basics*

Idea of the Day:

Gratitude is what opens
the spiritual doors to all the blessings...

EVERYTHING BECOMES CLEAR

GRIEF

Old..

S W A M I   S E Z

Waste not fresh tears
over old griefs

Today's Affirmation:

I have only joy and no sorrow...
about yesterday or tomorrow

Idea of the Day:

GROOVE
Get In The..

Get in the groove...
or you will find yourself in a rut

Today's Affirmation:

I'm "in the groove" and I link...
on time, on target, in sync

Idea of the Day:

"Man's mind once stretched by a new idea
never regains its original dimension"
— *Oliver Wendell Holmes*

GROWING
..Together Or Apart

Either you grow together...
or you grow apart
(To know... look within your heart)

Today's Affirmation:

I appreciate my relationships

Idea of the Day:

GUARANTEES

There are
no guarantees in life*

Today's Affirmation:

*I CAN guarantee that there is a
50/50 chance of anything occurring

Idea of the Day:

Safe bet:
There is a 50/50 chance
that it will rain tomorrow

GUIDANCE

..Through Spirit

S W A M I S E Z

Trust the spirit inside you...
and let the spirit guide you

Today's Affirmation:

*I trust the spirit of love and right action inside me...
to direct and guide me*

Idea of the Day:

There is one light
but many lamps

GUILT TRIPS

No guilt trips will be taken...
If you need a short trip, take a trip to the mall,
go bowling or go play pinball

Today's Affirmation:

My life is a "trip!"

Idea of the Day:

Forgive and live*!!*

HANGOVERS

The wrath
of grapes

Today's Affirmation:

*I believe in moderation
in all things*

Idea of the Day:

Today is Paul McCartney's birthday
(June 18, 1942)
In the Sixties Paul wrote
"Will you still need me, will you still feed me…
when I'm sixty-four"
On June 18, 2006, Paul turned 64

One Idea Can Change Your World

HAPPINESS
Achieving..

The surest way to make yourself happy...
is to make someone else happy

Today's Affirmation:

My present happiness is all I see...
I see all things as I would have them be

Idea of the Day:

As you focus on what you are grateful for...
your unhappiness will disappear

"One thing I know:
The only ones among you who will be really happy
are those who will have sought
and found how to serve"
— *Albert Schweitzer*

Happiness can be thought, taught and caught...
but not bought

One Idea Can Change Your World

HAPPINESS
..And Money

Money can't buy happiness...
but somehow it's more comfortable
to cry in a Porsche than in a Hyundai

Today's Affirmation:

I am grateful for my money...
as I am grateful for jokes that are funny!

Idea of the Day:

The happiness of your life
depends upon the quality
of your thoughts

HAPPINESS
Daily..

S W A M I S E Z

If you were happy every day of your life, you wouldn't be a human being... you'd be a Game Show Host

---

Today's Affirmation:

I am happy I am not Alex Trebek

Idea of the Day:

"Happiness is when
what you think, what you say
and what you do are in harmony"
— *Mahatma Gandhi*

"The more you share your happiness with others...
the more you have yourself"
— *Maxwell Maltz*

One Idea Can Change Your World

HAPPINESS
Formula For..

S W A M I S E Z

Do what you love...
and love what you do
*(Perfect happiness occurs
in the absence of striving for happiness)*

Today's Affirmation:

*I love what I do...
and I do what I love*

Idea of the Day:

The happiest people are those who are too busy to notice

Happiness is a way of travel...
not a destination

*Today is the Summer Solstice:
When it comes to getting a suntan...
ignorance is blister*

One Idea Can Change Your World

JUNE 23

HAPPINESS
Gift Of..

S W A M I S E Z

The gift of happiness
belongs to those who unwrap it
(If happiness forgets you for a little bit... never completely forget about it)

Today's Affirmation:

I am happier
than a tornado in a trailer park

Idea of the Day:

Today is Johannes Gutenberg's birthday
(June 23, 1400)
Write on *!!!*

HAPPINESS
Key to..

Looking for the key to happiness...??
The door is already open --
Come on in !!

Today's Affirmation:

Happiness is at the core...
I walk through the open door

Idea of the Day:

"Happiness can be achieved
through the systematic training of our hearts and minds...
through reshaping our attitudes and outlook
The key to happiness is in your own hands"
— *Dalai Lama*

"Happiness is a perfume you can't pour on others
without getting a few drops on yourself"
— *Ralph Waldo Emerson*

Today is Norman Cousins' birthday
(June 24, 1915)
"Hearty laughter is a good way to jog internally
without having to go outdoors"

HAPPINESS
Singing Your Way To..

S W A M I   S E Z

"Oh, what a beautiful morning, Oh what a beautiful day...I've got a wonderful feeling... everything's going my way"
—*Oscar Hammerstein*

Today's Affirmation:

I sing my favorite song from my favorite show...
and suddenly I feel happy and rarin' to go

Idea of the Day:

"There is only one way to happiness
and that is to cease worrying about things
which are beyond the power of our will"
– *Epictetus*

"He who sings scares away his woes"
– *Spanish Proverb*

"The happiness of your life
depends on the quality of your thoughts"
– *Marcus Aurelius*

JUNE 26

HAPPINESS
Source Of..

S W A M I   S E Z

Some pursue happiness...
others create it
(Your happiness: Deal or No-Deal ??)

Today's Affirmation:

I create that which makes me happy
and I create enough time...for an afternoon "nappy"

Idea of the Day:

"When one door of happiness closes...another opens
but often we look so long at the closed door that
we do not see the one which has been opened for us"
— *Helen Keller*

"Happiness belongs to the self-sufficient"
— *Aristotle*

JUNE 27

HAPPENING?!?
What's..

What's happening within... will create what's happening without

Something wonderful is happening to me...right here and right now !!
(I feel myself go into a effortless state of flow)

"An invasion of armies can be resisted...
but not an idea whose time has come"
— *Victor Hugo*

HAPPY
Color Yourself..

S   W   A   M   I   S   E   Z

"Most folks are about as happy as they make up their minds to be"
— Abraham Lincoln

T o d a y ' s   A f f i r m a t i o n :

When I'm depressed, and got the "downies..."
Love those delicious Swami Sez BROWNIES !!! (see recipe on page 368)

I d e a   o f   t h e   D a y :

Today is Mel Brook's birthday
(June 28,1926)
Mel Brooks has won all the great awards:
Emmy, Grammy, Oscar and Tony...
Mel Brooks is a funny guy !!

Go to Blockbuster and check out
one of his famous comedies
that are listed in the AFI
(American Film Institute's)
TOP 100 COMEDIES OF ALL TIME:
The Producers (#11) / Young Frankenstein (#13) / Blazing Saddles (#16)

Laugh yourself well !!!
(See the complete list of Top 100 Movie Comedies on pages 370-371)

O n e   I d e a   C a n   C h a n g e   Y o u r   W o r l d

HARD WORK

S W A M I S E Z

Hard work pays off in the future...
Laziness pays off now

Today's Affirmation:

I put my heart into my work....
and it pays off in spades

Idea of the Day:

The journey of a thousand sites...
begins with a single click

HEART
Healing Your..

To heal your own heart...
help mend someone else's
("No matter what our heartache may be...
laughing helps you forget it for a few seconds")
— Red Skelton

Today's Affirmation:
You can't heal... what you can't feel *
Reach out...reach out and touch someone

Idea of the Day:

"The great book is within your heart —
Open the pages of this inexhaustible book:
the source of all knowledge... you will know everything"
— Sivananda

* Affirm this now:
"The cells of my body radiate with vitality"

LOVE IS THE GREATEST HEALER OF ALL

JULY 1

<u>HELL</u>
If You Are Going Through..

S W A M I   S E Z

If you are going through hell,
keep going...
no need to stop and build a condo there *!!*

Today's Affirmation:

I am grateful and I know my worth...
Today I am living in heaven on earth

Idea of the Day:

"The mind in its own place
and in itself
can make a heaven of hell...
a hell of heaven"
— *John Milton*

Out of any chaos...

YOU CAN CREATE HARMONY

One Idea Can Change Your World

HERE
..And Now

S W A M I   S E Z

Welcome to the instantaneous HERE and the ever-present NOW

Today's Affirmation:

I am now here... here and now

Idea of the Day:

House of Yoga:
"Om" Sweet "Om"

HOLDING ON

S W A M I   S E Z

The hardest part of holding on is...
letting go

(Give it not... another thought)

Today's Affirmation:

I LET GO...
and let God

Idea of the Day:

If you hold on to ill-will
you will get ill...

To get well
be well-intentioned

HUMAN
Its only..

S W A M I S E Z

Be a human being...
doing a human doing

Today's Affirmation:

I AM this — and I DO that
Today's the Fourth of July… and I celebrate my freedom !!

Idea of the Day:

Today is Rube Goldberg's birthday
(July 4, 1883)
Think of something wildly inventive today…
then go watch fireworks *!!*

Rube Goldberg's Inventions

HUMOR
Multiplying..

S W A M I   S E Z

Humor multiplies through "mirthamatics"
$$(ha^2 \times ha^2 = hahahaha)$$
(Humor is simply a funny way of being serious)

Today's Affirmation:

Ha Ha Ha Ha
Ha Ha Ha Ha x 2 (...and repeat)

Idea of the Day:

Today is P.T. Barnum's birthday
(July 5, 1810)
Be the World's Greatest Showman that you can be *!!*

The charm of a chuckle... the snap of a snicker:
Humor can help you cope with *anything*...
Have you tickled your funny bone today??

"Laughter is inner jogging..."
— *Norman Cousins*

One Idea Can Change Your World

HUMOR
Sense Of..

Humor tickles the brain... laughter scratches it
*(Create a lifesyle in which humor is a
conscious and significant element)*

Today's Affirmation:

*I have a belief in comic relief...
I can laugh at myself and eliminate grief*

Idea of the Day:

When a thing is funny... search it for a hidden truth
— *George Bernard Shaw*

Today is the Dalai Lama's birthday
(July 6, 1935)
"If you want *others* to be happy... practice compassion
If *you* want to be happy... practice compassion"

HVNGER
Recognizing..

S   W   A   M   I   S   E   Z

When the clouds start to look
like mashed potatoes...
it's time to eat

Today's Affirmation:

I hunger for delicious clues from nature

Idea of the Day:

I AM
What..

S W A M I S E Z

What I am to be...
I am now becoming

Today's Affirmation:

I am that I am...
inventive by choice... and attentive to the inner voice

Idea of the Day:

I am more like I am now than I ever was before

Today is the birthday of John D. Rockefeller
(July 8, 1839)

Be rich in spirit
and you will be fabulously wealthy

One Idea Can Change Your World

IDEALS

S W A M I S E Z

Keep your ideals high enough to inspire you... and low enough to encourage you

---

Today's Affirmation:

I am inspired to greatness by my ideals

Idea of the Day:

Today is Nicola Tesla's birthday
(July 9, 1856)
Let the inventor and visionary that you are
come out and express

you will surprise yourself
with your own talent

One Idea Can Change Your World

IDEAS
Bad..

"It's such a beautiful day,
I think I'll skip my medications"

Did that doctor say:
"MEDICATE twice a day" or "MEDITATE twice a day?"

Today's Affirmation:

I recognize bad ideas...
(and I remember to take my prescriptions)

Idea of the Day:

Who's idea was it
to put an "s" in the word "lisp?"

ILLUMINATION

To illuminate the darkness... make light of it

Today's Affirmation:

*To counter the darkness...
I light a candle or carry a flashlight*

Idea of the Day:

Books:
"A drop of ink may make a million think"
— *Lord Byron*

IMAGINATION

It's Your..

S W A M I S E Z

Why imagine a bungalow...
when you can imagine a palace
(o r   a   g e o d e s i c   d o m e ?)

Today's Affirmation:

I stretch my imagination... and experience elation

Idea of the Day:

The power of imagination is the most abundant resource on the planet
mine it... and make it *yours*

"Imagination is the true magic carpet"
— *Norman Vincent Peale*

"Put something silly in the world that ain't been there before"
— *Shel Silverstein*

Today is Buckminster Fuller's birthday
(July 12, 1895)
"Welcome to 'SPACESHIP EARTH'...here's the controls"

One Idea Can Change Your World

IMMORTALITY

S W A M I   S E Z

Live forever:
so far... so good !!

Today's Affirmation:

I live each day forever

Idea of the Day:

"Frame your mind to mirth and merriment
which bar a thousand harms and lengthen life"
— *William Shakespeare*

"It may very well bring about immortality...
but it will take forever to test it"

One Idea Can Change Your World

INDUSTRIOUSNESS
(Versus Doing Nothing)

Doing nothing is tiring...
because you can't stop to rest

Today's Affirmation:

I'm constructive and productive

Idea of the Day:

Today is Woodie Guthrie's birthday
(July 14, 1912)
"This land is your land
this land is my land…"

Do *your* part to make this land
a better place for you and me

INSIGHT

S W A M I S E Z

Close your eyes
keep reading...

Vision is the art of seeing things invisible...
I can "see" with my eyes closed

Idea of the Day:

Today is Rembrandt's birthday
(July 15, 1606)
Rembrandt, possibly the greatest painter in European art history
suffered from stereo blindness…
He learned how to "see more" with his eyes closed, too

One Idea Can Change Your World

©2006 Church of Truth Through Humor / Swami Sez Press / B.E.Singer. All Rights Reserved

197

INSPIRATION
Well of..

S   W   A   M   I   S   E   Z

Go to the well of inspiration...
and experience deep wellness

Today's Affirmation:

I go to the well of inspiration...
and I am inspired

Idea of the Day:

It all starts with an idea...
you could say something brilliant at any moment

Inspiration cannot be willed... but it can be wooed

To bring it to fruition... listen to your intuition

INSTANTANAITY

S W A M I   S E Z

Whoop...
There it IS !!

Today's Affirmation:

I can get instant results... as long as I am patient
I can get instant results... as long as I am patient
I can get instant results... as long as I am patient

Idea of the Day:

"I am more of a sponge
than an inventor —
I absorb ideas from every source...
my principal business is giving
commercial value to the brilliant
but misdirected ideas of others"
— *Thomas Edison*

One Idea Can Change Your World

INSTANT MILLIONAIRE
How To Be An..

"Buy a million hats for $1...
and sell them for two dollars"
— *Robert E. Singer*

Today's Affirmation:

I am worthy to be a millionaire

Idea of the Day:

INTENTIONS

Clear..

You are a jewel of clarity and insight

Today's Affirmation:

I can see clearly now... the rain is gone...
It's gonna' be a bright, bright sunshiny day

Idea   of   the   Day:

"The act of contemplation creates the thing contemplated"
— *Isaac D'Israeli*

I know people charging $5,000
...and they are getting it

I know people charging $500
...and they are getting it

I know people charging zero
...and they are getting it *!!*

INTOLERANCE

Intolerance will not be tolerated

Today's Affirmation:

I am tolerant and a soother... and my life runs smoother

Idea of the Day:

INVEST
..In Yourself

S W A M I   S E Z

Invest in yourself...
and double your return

Today's Affirmation:

I am my own best investment

Idea of the Day:

Today is Marshall McLuhan's birthday
(July 21, 1911)
May you be inspired by the
"light bulb icon" above
to a clearly bright idea *!!*

Marshall McLuhan in the computer age:
"The modem is the message"

INVESTMENTS
Optimists vs. Pessimists

A lot of people become pessimists...
from financing optimists

Today's Affirmation:

When it comes to time and money...
I choose my investments well

Idea of the Day:

"The best investment
is in tools of one's own trade"
— *Benjamin Franklin*

ISSUES
Dwelling On..

S W A M I   S E Z

If you've got an issue...
here's a tissue

Today's Affirmation:

I remember not to make a drama out of my issue...
It IS what it IS

Idea of the Day:

"It's always somethin'*!*
and if it's not one thing... it's another*!!*"
— *Roseanne Roseannadanna*

JOB
..Appreciation

You can whine because you have to go to work...
or you can shout for joy because
you have a job to go to

Today's Affirmation:

Yay, work!!

Idea of the Day:

There are two kinds of people in life:
People who like their job...
and people who don't work there any more

JOB
Keeping Your..

The only person who can be consistently wrong and still keep his job...is the weatherman

(think it'll rain ??)

Today's Affirmation:

*I am diligent
to the task before me*

Idea of the Day:

JOB?
Need A..

Go to a "hire" source

I look to "hire consciousness"
and I naturally transition… to the perfect position

Idea of the Day:

Today is Mick Jagger's birthday
(July 26, 1943)
"If you start me up
start me up, start me up
I'll never stop…"

JOB IS A DOG

How To Know If You're..

S W A M I S E Z

If you're just scratchin' to get by... and itchin' to be somewhere else

Today's Affirmation:

*I vow to not work in an animal clinic...
if I don't like cats and dogs*

Idea of the Day:

Help wanted: Telepath
You know where to apply

Finding your calling:
If endless calling doesn't call to you,
scratch telemarketing off your list

Career tip:
If you would have done it for free...
that career is meant to be

One Idea Can Change Your World

JOY
Experiencing..

S W A M I S E Z

Joy to the world
Joy to the fishes in the deep blue sea
Okay... *joy for you, too!!*

Today's Affirmation:

I and the world are as one...
and deep joy has just begun

Idea of the Day:

"One person's burden can be another person's joy"
— *Dr. Rhonda Clifton Lyons*

"One joy scatters a hundred griefs"
— *Chinese Proverb*

"At the touch of love everyone becomes a poet"
"Roses are red, violets are blue..."
— *Plato / Bobby Vinton*

KARAOKE
Healing Through..

S W A M I   S E Z

When things go wrong...
start singing a song!

Today's Affirmation:

A one and a two and a......

Idea of the Day:

KINDNESS

If you were arrested for kindness...
would there be enough evidence to convict you?

Today's Affirmation:

Each day I find... something to do that is kind

Idea of the Day:

Today is Arnold Schwarzenegger's birthday
(July 30, 1947)
Be the "terminator"
of all negative thoughts

KINDNESS
Developing..

S W A M I S E Z

Practice random acts of kindness everyday
(Be kind...and you will find...peace of mind)

Today's Affirmation:

*I practice random acts of kindness every day
and take time to smell the roses... along the way*

Idea of the Day:

Today is J.K. Rowling's birthday
(July 31, 1965)
She went from homeless
to being a billionaire
Be creative !!
As you conceive
so can you receive

One Idea Can Change Your World

LAUGH
Time To..

An average person laughs over 15 times a day...
what are you waiting for???
(Seven days without laughter makes one weak)

Today's Affirmation:

*I find the humor in most any situation
and I laugh heartily... no matter the agitation*

Idea of the Day:

Start laughing at a stressful situation...
and your brain is no longer able
to concentrate on negative thoughts

"Laughter is an instant vacation"
— *Milton Berle*

"At the height of laughter...
the universe is flung into a
kaleidoscope of new possibilities"
— *Jean Houston*

Every day is World Laughter Day...
TIME TO CELEBRATE !!

One Idea Can Change Your World

LAUGHING
..At Yourself

S W A M I   S E Z

Blessed are those who can laugh at themselves...
for they shall never cease to be amused
("Laughter is the best medicine in the world")
— *Milton Berle*

Today's Affirmation:

I can laugh at myself... hey, what's so funny??

Idea of the Day:

"What soap is to the body
laughter is to the soul"
— *Yiddish Proverb*

"Life is too important
to be taken seriously"
— *Oscar Wilde*

You're on the way to being cured
the day you have your first real laugh... at yourself

One Idea Can Change Your World

LAUGHTER
Value Of..

"A good hearty laugh is worth a thousand groans"
("We don't laugh because we're happy...we're happy because we laugh")
— *William James*

Today's Affirmation:

*I laugh a hearty laugh at what is seemingly bad...
and suddenly my heart feels glad*

Idea of the Day:

Laugh and the whole world laughs with you:
"Laughter is the closest distance between two people"
— *Victor Borge*

They laughed at Einstein
They laughed at the Wright Brothers
But they also laughed at Bozo the Clown

At least 100 times a season... laugh for no reason

LAUGH YOURSELF WELL
..Naturally

S W A M I S E Z

Practice "Ho-Ho-Holistic" Medicine
for ultimate "Hee-Hee-Hee Healing..."
Do your part to cure the dearth of mirth on earth
(He who laughs...lasts)

Today's Affirmation:

I know that laughter is the best medicine

Idea of the Day:

"He deserves paradise who makes his companions laugh"
— The Koran

The more you give... The more you get
The more you laugh... The less you fret

Laughter is jam on the toast of life

Join the Laughter Movement... check out www.laughteryoga.org

(Tell 'em Swami sent you)

One Idea Can Change Your World

LAW
..Of Attraction

S   W   A   M   I   S   E   Z

The Law of Attraction...
is always in action
(Follow your bliss)

T o d a y ' s   A f f i r m a t i o n :

I obey the law of attraction...
for maximum satisfaction

I d e a   o f   t h e   D a y :

Experience the awesome power of your mind

Supply yourself with a mental equivalent...
and the thing must come to you

Think it... send it... let it go... and it will be yours

LAW
..Of Close Encounters

S W A M I S E Z

The probability of meeting someone you know increases when you are with someone you don't want to be seen with

Today's Affirmation:

Life is a treat...
and I am discreet

Idea of the Day:

Today is Andy Worhol's birthday
(August 6, 1911)
Soup for the soul:
"In the future
everyone will be famous
for fifteen minutes"

LAW
..Of Instantaneity

S W A M I   S E Z

No matter where you go...
there you are!!

(No sooner "said" than "done" — just like "magic")

Today's Affirmation:

I am where I am

Idea of the Day:

Relax...
Obey Nature's Law
Quit resisting a rest

Cole's Law:
Slice cabbage thinly

LEADERSHIP
Ultimate..

S W A M I S E Z

Lead, follow...
or get out of the way!!

Today's Affirmation:

*I know when to follow and know when to lead
and when to get out of the way... as the occasion may need*

Idea of the Day:

"Without a shepherd... sheep are not a flock"
— *Russian Proverb*

"The speed of the leader
determines the rate of the pack"
— *Phil McLeod*

The difference between
a boss and a leader:
A boss says "Go!"
A leader says
"Let's go!"

One Idea Can Change Your World

LEARNING

Learn from the mistakes of others...
you can't live long enough to make them all yourself

Today's Affirmation:

From what I read, observe and people say...
I learn something new each and every day

Idea of the Day:

Of the positive that you learn
PASS IT ON
Each one... Teach one

LEARNING
A Little..

A little learning is a dangerous thing...
(but a lot of ignorance is worse)

Today's Affirmation:

Today I yearn to learn

Idea of the Day:

"The eagle never lost so much time
as when he submitted to learn from the crow"
— *William Blake*

LET GO!!!

S W A M I S E Z

The longer you carry a problem...
the heavier it gets

(Whatever it is, JUST LET IT GO... and let the river flow:
Be the road...and let the traffic go by)

Today's Affirmation:

Today I let go of my problem and any attachment to final results...
The Universe says, "Thank you" and I say, "No problem!"

Idea of the Day:

Levity helps us
rise to the occasion

Nothing is important
(why give importance to nothing?)

AUGUST 12

LETTING NATURE
..Run Its Course

S W A M I S E Z

The sun will set without your help
—Old Yiddish saying
(What the caterpillar calls the end of the world...
the butterfly knows otherwise)

Today's Affirmation:

I know that nature will run its course without my assistance...
I relax and "float downstream" without resistance

Idea of the Day:

"The natural healing force in each one of us
is the greatest force in getting well"
— Hippocrates

Today is George Hamilton's birthday
(August 12, 1939)
A great day to get a tan

One Idea Can Change Your World

LEVITY
Lightening Up

Levity
overcomes
gravity

Today's Affirmation:

I lighten up and see the light...
with joy and clarity... I "be the light"

Idea of the Day:

Humor makes one's problems seem trivial

Today is Don Ho's birthday
(August 13, 1930)
"Tiny Bubbles…
make me feel happy
make me feel fine"

LIFE
Applying Computer Principles To..

S   W   A   M   I   S   E   Z

If you think you've messed up your life...
just press 'Ctrl Alt Delete'
and start all over

Today's Affirmation:

Today I "kick myself in the rear..."
and re-boot my life to "clear"

Idea of the Day:

Life is 5% of what happens to you
and 95% of how you respond to it

LIFE
..Appreciation

SWAMI SEZ

"Nice to be here...
nice to be *anywhere*"
— *Dèjá Vu of Keith Richards*
The Rolling Stones

Today's Affirmation:

I appreciate wherever I am

Idea of the Day:

Life is a trip... enjoy your vacation

Each of us brings our own sound
to the orchestra of life

Live life to the foolist...
find humor in all things

LIFE
Being Right About Your..

S W A M I S E Z

Live every day like it's your last...
because one day, you'll be right !!

Today's Affirmation:

I live every day to its fullest

Idea of the Day:

There is one life and it is your life.... RIGHT NOW *!!*

Life cannot withhold itself from you...
Life is fully given to you to enjoy

Today is Madonna's birthday
(August 16, 1958)
"...that consciousness is everything
and that all things begin with a thought...
We are responsible for our own fate
We reap what we sow
We get what we give
We pull in what we put out
I know these things for sure"

One Idea Can Change Your World

LIFE
Deposits And Withdrawals

S W A M I S E Z

You withdraw nothing out of life...
except what you deposit into it

Today's Affirmation:

I do my banking...
then I do my thanking

Idea of the Day:

"Life is a grindstone...
Whether it grinds you down or polishes you up
depends on what you're made of"
— *Jacob M. Braude*

Today is Mae West's birthday
(August 17, 1893)
"Why don't you come up and see me sometime!"

LIFE
..Is Like A "Cheers Bar"

S W A M I   S E Z

If you live in you own little world...
at least they know you there

Today's Affirmation:

I emerge from my own little world
to experience the glory of the universe unfurled

Idea of the Day:

You can write the script
and produce the scenes
that make up your life

Life is a state of mind:
Imagine the one you want...
and then create it

LIFE
..Is Like A Frank Sinatra Record

S W A M I S E Z

What goes around... comes around
("That's life...that's what all the people say...
You're riding high in April, shot down in May...")

Today's Affirmation:

If I am down, I know I can't go wrong...
listening to a Frank Sinatra song

Idea of the Day:

To do is to be (Descartes)
To be is to do (Voltaire)
Do be do be do (Sinatra)

Today is Gene Roddenberry's birthday
(August 19, 1921)
"Boldly go where no man has gone before"

One Idea Can Change Your World

LIFE
..Is Like A Garden

S W A M I S E Z

Life is like a garden...
DIG IT !!

Today's Affirmation:

I know it is my nature to grow

Idea of the Day:

Nip any negative thoughts in the bud...
before they bloom into a thorny bush

LIFE
..Is Like An Oreo Cookie

S   W   A   M   I   S   E   Z

Enjoy the "hi-de-highs"
the "low-de-lows..."
and the creamy middles

Today's Affirmation:

I enjoy life like an Oreo Cookie...
In fact, I think I'll have one right now... better yet, I think I'll have a brownie!!

Idea of the Day:

Not one shred of evidence
supports the notion that life is serious

LIFE

..Is Like Money

S W A M I S E Z

Yesterday: a cancelled check
Tomorrow: a promissory note
Today: cash in hand – spend it wisely!!

Today's Affirmation:

I spend my "time and dime" wisely:
Whether I am rich or poor... it's nice to have money

Idea of the Day:

Today is Ray Bradbury's birthday
(August 22, 1920)
"I don't try to describe the future
I try to prevent it"

One Idea Can Change Your World

LIFE
..Is Like A Raffle

Life is like a raffle...
you must be present to win

---

*I know that to win and for them to pick it
I must do my part... and at least buy a ticket*

Idea of the Day:

LIFE
..Is Like Surfing

S W A M I S E Z

Surf life!!

Today's Affirmation:

When life gives me an ocean of emotion
Toes to the nose... I ride one wave at a time

Idea of the Day:

LIFE
Secret Of..

S W A M I S E Z

The secret of life...
is that there *is* no secret *!!*

Today's Affirmation:

Today... I now know life's secret

Idea of the Day:

"Life is what we make it...
Always has been
Always will be"
— *Grandma Moses*

Life is like a Star Trek Episode...
"Beam me up, Scottie"

LIFE
Your..

S W A M I S E Z

Life is not measured by the breaths you take...
rather by the moments that take your breath away
(Life is a journey... not a destination)

Today's Affirmation:

Right now I feel a flow of Energy, Light and Love
filling my entire being

Idea of the Day:

The adventure of life:
Like always...like never before

If your whole life is unusual
and you had a usual experience...
that would be very unusual

Life vibrates...

Enjoy good vⁱbraTioNs //

LIFE
Your Lot In..

S W A M I   S E Z

If it's *YOUR LOT* in life...
build something on it
(Go where there is no path... and leave a trail)

T o d a y ' s   A f f i r m a t i o n :

Today I build something on the fertile soil of my imagination

I d e a   o f   t h e   D a y :

Today is Mother Teresa's birthday
(August 27, 1910)
Winner of the Nobel Peace Prize
"To keep a lamp burning
we have to keep putting oil in it"

One Idea Can Change Your World

LIFE
Zest For Life

S W A M I S E Z

Life is very kind...
because it gives you just one day at a time
(Life is what you make it...make it a great one!!)

Today's Affirmation:

*I have a zest for life... and overcome any strife
because I take "just O-N-E day at a time"*

Idea of the Day:

Today is Leo Tolstoy's birthday
(August 28, 1828)
"Everyone thinks of changing the world
but no one thinks of changing himself"

LIMB
Out On A..

As a tree is bent...
so it will grow

Today's Affirmation:

*I am guided and nurtured
by the forces of nature*

Idea of the Day:

LIMITATIONS

Accept your limitations...
and you can go beyond them
(Act as though you are... and you will be)

Today's Affirmation:

I focus on every success I have ever had, no matter the size or kind...
I relive each success until it becomes vivid in my mind

Idea of the Day:

Today is Warren Buffett's birthday
(August 30, 1930)
"It's only when the tide goes out
that you discover who's been swimming naked"

LITERATE
Congratulations On Being..

Nearly half the population never reads books
If you are reading this, congratulations....
you are the other half !!

Today's Affirmation:

*I find wisdom, knowledge and enjoyment
In all that I read*

Idea of the Day:

"Outside of a dog, a book is a man's best friend
Inside of a dog, it's too hard to read"
— Groucho Marx

Today is Maria Montessori's birthday
(August 31, 1870)
"The greatest sign of success for a teacher
is to be able to say 'the children are now working
as if I did not exist'"

LIVING
..Each Moment

S W A M I S E Z

Live your life as if your life depended on it

Today's Affirmation:

*Today I live each moment
to the fullest*

Idea of the Day:

Internal alignment... brings life refinement

Today is "Dr. Phil" McGraw's birthday
(September 1, 1950)
"Sometimes you just got to give yourself
what you wish someone else
would give you"

LIVING LIFE
..Like A Da Vinci

S W A M I S E Z

Let each day
be your *masterpiece*

My life is my canvas...
and I am the artist

Idea of the Day:

LOOKS
(Instant Improvement)

S W A M I   S E Z

Smile:
an inexpensive way to instantly
improve your looks

T o d a y ' s   A f f i r m a t i o n :

I smile from ear to ear...
and bring forth instant cheer

I d e a   o f   t h e   D a y :

LOSS
How To Deal With..

S W A M I S E Z

If you lose...
don't lose the lesson
(For every loss there exists a corresponding gain)

Today's Affirmation:

Sometimes I win and sometimes I lose...
How I take it... is how I choose

Idea of the Day:

LOVE
Falling In..

If you're not ready to *fall in love...* just *lean* a little bit
(Love can be a "comedy of Eros")

Today's Affirmation:

I love life, I love who I love... and I love a good brownie
(see Swami Sez Brownie Recipe on page 368)

Idea of the Day:

Don't marry the person you think you can live with...
marry the person you think you can't live without

Love is the magician that pulls magic out of its own hat

Today is Raquel Welch's birthday
(September 5, 1940)
Upon receiving Best Visual Effects Oscar:
"My name is Raquel Welch
I am here for Visual Effects
and I have two of them"

One Idea Can Change Your World

LOVING YOURSELF
Commitment To..

S W A M I   S E Z

Do you really love yourself...
or are you just fooling around

T o d a y ' s   A f f i r m a t i o n :

I find total satisfaction...
knowing that my life is expressing love in action

I d e a   o f   t h e   D a y :

Ultimately...
Love is everything

Love is the greatest healer of all...
Better to have loved a short girl
than never to have loved a tall

LUNCH
Let's Do..

Your next success is sometimes just a *"Let's do lunch"* away!!

Today's Affirmation:

*I "break bread" with
like-minded people*

Idea of the Day:

Do what you love
(and the money will follow)

MAGIC INCANTATION
..To Make Problems Go Away

SWAMI SEZ

"Ooga Booga!!"

Today's Affirmation:

My problems disappear like magic

Idea of the Day:

ABRA CADABRA:
"I create as I speak"

ABRACADABRA
ABRACADABR
ABRACADAB
ABRACADA
ABRACAD
ABRACA
ABRAC
ABRA
ABR
AB
A

MARRIAGE SAVER
Ultimate..

**"I was wrong, you are right
I love you...
*(What was I thinking ??)"***

Today's Affirmation:

*I know just what to say,
at just the right time… in just the right way*

Idea of the Day:

Whoever thinks that marriage
is a 50/50 proposition
doesn't know the half of it

MATHEMATICS
..Of Happiness

Count your blessings!!

Today's Affirmation:

When I'm worried and I can't sleep
I count my blessings, instead of sheep

Idea of the Day:

If you had as many ideas
during the day
as when you had insomnia...
you would make a fortune

MAXIMIZING
..Your Capabilities

S W A M I S E Z

Whatever you are...
be a good one
—Abraham Lincoln

Today's Affirmation:

I am the best me...
I know how to be

Idea of the Day:

MILLION
You Are One-In-A..

If you are one-in-a-million and there are
6 billion people in the world...that means
there are 6,000 people out there just like you
(Your Mission: Go out and find them)

Today's Affirmation:

*I seek fellow one-in-a-million people...
and my life and the world becomes a better place*

Idea of the Day:

Today is Ruben Studdard's birthday
(September 12, 1978)
"I just never let anything bother me, man…
I know myself really well
Nobody's opinion of me
can shake my opinion of myself"

One Idea Can Change Your World

<u>MIND</u>
Like A Window

S   W   A   M   I   S   E   Z

Keep a window open in your mind
for new ideas
(If you don't use your mind... someone else will)

Today's Affirmation:

I open my mind...
and wonderment I find

Idea of the Day:

"Empty your mind...
Become still and everything will happen of its own accord
There is really nothing you have to do... just be still"
— *Robert Adams*

"To the mind that is still...the whole universe surrenders"
— *Chuang Tse*

"Every thought sets the fulfillment of its desire in motion in Mind...
and Mind sees the thing as already done"
— *Ernest Holmes*

One Idea Can Change Your World

MIRACLES
Secret of..

Miracles happen to those who believe in miracles
(To see a miracle... be a miracle)

Today's Affirmation:

I believe in miracles

Idea of the Day:

Love is the greatest of miracles...
It is the end and aim of everything
and the greatest
healing power
there is

MISTAKES
Learning From Your..

S   W   A   M   I   S   E   Z

You can learn from your mistakes...
be sure to make some
(You are making progress... if each mistake is a new one)

T o d a y ' s   A f f i r m a t i o n :

With each mistake I make...
I grow more conscious and awake

I d e a   o f   t h e   D a y :

"A man who has committed a mistake
and doesn't correct it...
is committing another mistake"
— *Confucius*

Today is Prince Harry's birthday
(September 15, 1984)
"Maybe it was a sign of my immaturity
Something like that I will never do again
It was a very stupid thing to do
and I've learned my lesson"

MOMENT

Appreciation For The..

SWAMI SEZ

Yesterday has gone,
Tomorrow may never come...
Experience the miracle of the NOW

Today's Affirmation:

*I appreciate
each moment*

Idea of the Day:

Today is B.B. King's birthday
(September 16, 1925)
In honor of the King of Blues...
"Hey... how about a delicious brownie ??"

MONEY
..vs. Chocolate

S W A M I   S E Z

Money talks...
chocolate sings!!

Today's Affirmation:

*I know there is nothing like good chocolate
(especially if it's part of a big chewy brownie... got milk?)*

Idea of the Day:

"I was born into it and there was nothing I could do about it
It was there, like air or food or any other element...
the only question with wealth is what you do with it"
— *John D. Rockefeller, Jr.*

"A rich man is nothing
but a poor man with money"
— *W.C. Fields*

They say money doesn't grow on trees...
(you have to beat the bushes for it)

*If money doesn't grow on trees...
why do banks have branches?*

One Idea Can Change Your World

MORNINGS
Good..

The proper response to "Good morning" is not "Prove it!"

Today's Affirmation:

"Zip a dee doo dah, zippity yay...
My, oh my, what a wonderful day!!"

Idea of the Day:

There's nothing like a good Disney tune
to lighten and brighten up a day

MOURNING
Positive..

SWAMI SEZ

Good
Grief
(One joy scatters a hundred griefs)

Today's Affirmation:

Though loved ones die and I may cry...
I am grateful for the memories of my loved one and I

Idea of the Day:

NAMES
Your Two..

You have two names:
the one you were born with...
and the one you make for yourself

Today's Affirmation:

Though many...
We are really only one

Idea of the Day:

NEGATIVE THOUGHTS

S W A M I   S E Z

Negative thoughts set you up for failure
and unhappiness... and that is *positively* so *!!*
(Apply the principles of photography... use the negative to develop)

T o d a y ' s   A f f i r m a t i o n :

The negative I refute — old beliefs I transmute
As I change my beliefs, I regulate the quality of my happiness... no dispute

I d e a   o f   t h e   D a y :

The ultimate solution for old "mental tapes..."
Erase and Replace

Negativity is often at the root
of a big dispute...
FIND THE POSITIVE

One Idea Can Change Your World

NEW BEGINNINGS

Starting with today's date... it's a brand new slate
(You know you're a pack rat...
when you come back from The Dump with more than you took)

Today's Affirmation:

I start from present date...
each day a fresh new slate

Idea of the Day:

"Only if your thoughts are quiet
and your heart at peace
can you be fully attentive and aware
of the unfolding moment"
— *A Spiritual Warrior*

If you have too much stuff...
sell the excess of what you own:
try a sell-a-bit lifestyle

NOW

S W A M I   S E Z

One of these days...
is *none* of these days
(Your personal patent is almost up... re-invent yourself!!)

T o ᴅ a y ' s   A f f i r m a t i o n :

With ease, I go from "nowhere..."
to "now here"

I ᴅ e a   o f   t h e   D a y :

"Realize deeply that the present moment is all you ever have"
— Eckhart Tolle

Today is Ray Charles' birthday
(September 23, 1930)
"You ask me what I'd like to do that I haven't done and I say 'Nothin'
I haven't any mountains to climb or oceans to swim
I've been an extremely blessed individual
I'm not clamorin' for more trinkets
If I were to die tomorrow
I could say
'I've had a good life'"

O n e   I ᴅ e a   C a n   C h a n g e   Y o u r   W o r l ᴅ

NOW
New..

Now is the beginning of the new beginning
(If not now, then when?... If not me, then who??)

Today's Affirmation:

*I know now that each moment...
is a new beginning*

Idea of the Day:

Living in the Now
is the wave of the future

"Be Here Now"

"Don't think about the future... just be here now
Don't think about the past...
just be here now

*(Why now?
Because it's too late to do it sooner)*

OBSTACLES

May all your obstacles recede into the distance
as quickly as the Burma-Shave signs used to
on the road to Las Vegas

Today's Affirmation:

In my journey along life's highway...
the signs along the way guide and amuse me

Idea of the Day:

OMNIPOTENCE

(Atheists and Agnostics Please Skip To Next Page)

S W A M I   S E Z

There is no spot...
where God is not

Today's Affirmation:

*I put my faith, as a matter of course...
in a Higher Source*

Idea of the Day:

Today is Jack La Lane's birthday
(September 26, 1914)
"If you haven't exercised in a long time
just start out for a couple of minutes a day
then work it up a little bit
You'll be surprised at the end of thirty days
how many things you are doing"

One Idea Can Change Your World

OPPORTUNITY
..Knockin'

S W A M I S E Z

If opportunity doesn't knock...
build a door!!
(When one door closes... another door opens)

Today's Affirmation:

"Get it... I think it's for you"

Idea of the Day:

The secret of life is to be ready when opportunity knocks

Even if opportunity knocks...
you still have to get off your seat
and open the door

Opportunities always look bigger going than coming

"A wise man will make more opportunities than he finds"
— *Sir Francis Bacon*

One Idea Can Change Your World

OPTIMISTS
..Versus Pessimists

S W A M I S E Z

A stumbling block to the pessimist...
is a stepping stone to the optimist

(When life gives you lemons... buy a shopping mall
and give yourself exclusive hot dog* and lemonade rights)

Today's Affirmation:

Along the path of life, I accentuate the positive...
and eliminate the negative

Idea of the Day:

*As I eat my hot dog
I relish every moment

PAST AND FUTURE
..And The Now

Let the past and future
worry about themselves...
Enjoy the now*!!*

Today's Affirmation:

Here I am right now:
I see the past as a place of reference... rather than a place of preference

Idea of the Day:

Awaken to who you are...
Conscious Presence

Hanging on to the past can feel good...
Sometimes it's only when you let go
that you can make room for the rest of your life to show up

Today is Jerry Lee Lewis' birthday
(September 29, 1935)
"I studied to be a preacher
but couldn't live up to what I was preaching
Too many good looking women out there
so I stuck with rock 'n' roll... What's your problem!"
(Jimmy Swaggart is Jerry Lee Lewis' cousin)

One Idea Can Change Your World

PATIENCE

Lord give me patience...
and give it to me now *!!!*

---

*I have the patience of a flea...who has its whole life
to just "crawl along the dog...crawl along the dog"*

Idea of the Day:

OCTOBER 1

PERFORMANCE
Peak..

S W A M I   S E Z

"If that don't get it...
It can't get got"
(Be "inner peace..." and allow all negative thoughts to cease)

Today's Affirmation:

*As I am Inner Peace...
all negative thoughts cease*

Idea of the Day:

Challenge yourself to be a different version of you...
a braver version, willing to grab joy
and take it for a spin

If I was a 12 cylinder Jaguar...
I would be running on all 12 cylinders

PERSISTENCE

Keep going...for success is just around the corner for those who refuse to quit
(If you fall down seven times... stand up eight)

If there is something I want and it's something I need...
I never fear and refuse to quit until I've done the deed

I d e a o f t h e D a y :

Today is Groucho Marx's birthday
(October 2, 1890)
"Those are my principles, and if you don't like them...
well, I have others"

PERSON
Purpose Of The Other..

SWAMI SEZ

The other person is just a reflection...
so you can see yourself better

Today's Affirmation:

*In the eyes of thee...
I see a reflection of me*

Idea of the Day:

PERSPECTIVE

Sometimes the most truth comes from seeing it from the other person's point of view

Today's Affirmation:

As I observe it from the other's point of view
I can quickly see what I must do

Idea of the Day:

What you see
is mainly dependent on
what you look for

Today is Alvin Toffler's birthday
(October 4, 1928)
From the Father of *Future Shock:*
"Change is the process by which
the future invades our lives"

PERSPECTIVE
Global..

S W A M I   S E Z

If things don't seem to be
going well for you today...remember,
it's already tomorrow in New Zealand

Today's Affirmation:

*To see from the Universal Consciousness...
I look to the world as a microcosm*

Idea of the Day:

One Idea Can Change Your World

PESSIMIST

Optimistic..

S W A M I S E Z

This is the best day...
of my miserable life

Today's Affirmation:

Though this day may be a mess...
this day I still do bless

Idea of the Day:

An Optimist sees the glass half full
A Pessimist sees the glass half empty
An Engineer sees the glass
as twice as big as it needs to be

Scientific fact:
Optimists live longer than Pessimists
BE AN OPTIMIST

OCTOBER 7

PIGEON-HOLING

S W A M I S E Z

The only thing that's supposed to fit
in a pigeon hole...
is another pigeon

Today's Affirmation:

I believe in Divine Order of my physical space:
I see things in their divine and perfect place

Idea of the Day:

One Idea Can Change Your World

PLANNING

S W A M I S E Z

Today is the tomorrow we should have been
planning for yesterday
(when it comes to planning...do some)

T o d a y ' s A f f i r m a t i o n :

I am a fan...
of a good plan

I d e a o f t h e D a y :

Never forget what you need to remember

Write it down
as soon as you think of it *!!*

PLANNING
Days And Nights

S W A M I   S E Z

For the happiest life...
Days should be rigorously planned
and nights left open to chance

Today's Affirmation:

I play it loose or tight...
depending on whether it's day or night

Idea of the Day:

Today is John Lennon's birthday
(October 9, 1940)
"If the Beatles or the 60's had a message
it was *Learn to swim and once you've learned*
SWIM ..."

PLEASURE
Finding..

Find pleasure...
in the pleasure of pleasing

Today's Affirmation:

I am supremely pleased when I please others...
for in pleasing others, I please myself

Idea of the Day:

POSITIVE

Positively..

S W A M I   S E Z

Find something positive
in positively everything that happens!!
(accentuate the positive...eliminate the negative)

T o d a y ' s   A f f i r m a t i o n :

Whatever it is...
I replace it with the mental equivalent of positivity and love

I d e a   o f   t h e   D a y :

You can't stay stuck
when your WD-40
is positivity

One Idea Can Change Your World

PRETENDING

SWAMI SEZ

Pretend life is a comedy...
and you're the main character

Today's Affirmation:

*I know all the world is a stage and all its inhabitants players...
today's show is a divine comedy!*

Idea of the Day:

PRIVACY
Best Time For..

When you're alone...
is a good time to give yourself
a little privacy

Today's Affirmation:

I take a break...
for its own sake

Idea of the Day:

Today is Lenny Bruce's birthday
(October 13, 1925)
"Every day people are straying away from the church
and going back to God"

PROBLEMS

S W A M I   S E Z

The best way to forget your own problems...
is to help someone else solve theirs
(if your problem is bigger than you...become bigger than it)

Today's Affirmation:

*When I have a problem, I help someone else with their problem...
and somehow my problem disappears*

Idea of the Day:

And you think you have problems:
The female praying mantis initiates sex
by ripping the male's head off

PROBLEMS
..At Night

Do not take problems to bed with you
(they hog the covers)

T o d a y ' s   A f f i r m a t i o n :

Each night as I enter my sacred sleeping chamber and walk across the floor
I leave the problems of the day... outside my bedroom door

I d e a   o f   t h e   D a y :

Maintain close communion with your true center...
and allow only positive thoughts to enter

"According to my calculations
the problem doesn't exist"
— *Higher Spirit*

PROBLEMS
Criteria For Solution

Make your problem like a flashlight: accessible... but not "on" all the time

(If you're invited to a seminar titled
"How to Turn Your Imaginary Problems Into Real Ones"... don't go !!)

Today's Affirmation:

If a problem should befall us...
call me "Speedy Gonzales"

Idea of the Day:

Persevere and never fear

Today is Noah Webster's birthday
(October 16, 1758)
It took Noah Webster 27 years to write his book
(This book took the author three years)
When Webster finished at the age of 70
his dictionary had 70,000 words in it
(There are "cornfields" and then there are "redwood forests")

Defining Noah Webster

PROBLEMS
Heavy..

S W A M I   S E Z

It doesn't matter how heavy your problem is...
it just matters how long you hold it
(LET GO: a problem is just a decision waiting to be made)

Today's Affirmation:

Why wait to lift the weight...
let go now before it's too late

Idea of the Day:

Today is Evel Knievel's birthday
(October 17, 1938)
"A Roman General in the time of Caesar made a motto:
If it is possible, it is done
If it is impossible... it WILL be done
And that, ladies and gentlemen
is what I live by"

PROBLEMS
How To Escape Your..

S W A M I   S E Z

Practice the "Power of Now"
(There IS no problem in the instantaneous now
I face it... and erase it)

T o d a y ' s   A f f i r m a t i o n :

I find the "WOW"...in the "NOW!!!"
and I give my problems the ol' "heave ho-ho-ho!!"

I d e a   o f   t h e   D a y :

Problems need the past and future to survive...
JUST BE PRESENT

There's something within ourselves...
to get us out of ourselves

Today is Chuck Berry's birthday
(October 18,1926)
"Roll over Beethoven
and tell Tchaikovsky the news"

PROBLEMS
Orderly Dealing With..

S W A M I   S E Z

Though they refuse to get in line...
address your problems one at a time
(Problems are really disguised opportunities)

Today's Affirmation:

*I step outside my problem and analyze it as if I am
an impartial observer... and I gain a new positive perspective*

Idea of the Day:

WHEN DID
YOU FIRST
BECOME
AWARE OF
THIS PROBLEM?

WHAT
PROBLEM?

I do not own my problem...
I'm just renting it for a while 'til it can teach me its lesson

One Idea Can Change Your World

PROCRASTINATION
"Island Of Tomorrow"

S W A M I   S E Z

"Someday Isle..."
(Procrastinate now...why put it off ??)

Today's Affirmation:

"One of these days" is "none of these days"
DO IT NOW !!!

Idea of the Day:

Today is Art Buchwald's birthday
(October 20, 1925)
"You can't make up anything anymore...
The world itself is a satire
All you're doing is
recording it"

One Idea Can Change Your World

PROFESSIONAL HELP
When It's Time To Get..

S W A M I S E Z

When your Rice Crispies start talking to you...
and it's making sense

(or you take the cereal from the cupboard and eat the box for extra fiber)

Today's Affirmation:

I am confident that "snap, crackle, pop"
has no special meaning

Idea of the Day:

If you eat regular Rice Crispies with chocolate milk...
will it taste the same as eating Co-Co Crispies with regular milk??

Today is Alfred Nobel's Birthday
(October 21, 1833)
"Hope is nature's veil
for hiding truth's nakedness"

One Idea Can Change Your World

PROSPERITY
Reading For..

Find out what the poor people are reading
(...and don't read that stuff)

Today's Affirmation:

I pattern my life after winners

Idea of the Day:

QVIET
Keeping..

S   W   A   M   I   S   E   Z

A closed mouth...
gathers no feet

T o d a y ' s   A f f i r m a t i o n :

If I have nothing to say...
I say nothing

I d e a   o f   t h e   D a y :

Today is Johnny Carson's birthday
(October 23, 1925)
Carnac the Magnificent and Swami Sez
are the ultimate in wisdom and humor
under any one turban

"Carnac the Magnificent"   "Swami Sez"

REACHING
..For The Moon

S W A M I S E Z

Reach for the moon...
if you fall short, you'll still be
among the stars

Today's Affirmation:

I strive to the furthest level of achievement
(to the moon and beyond)

Idea of the Day:

Tonight...
look up to the skies and
BE INSPIRED

REALITY
..And Change

Seeing and accepting reality...
is the first step toward changing it

Today's Affirmation:

"Nothing is real...
and nothing to get hung about"

Idea of the Day:

Despite our judgments, reality happens anyway

Okay...who stopped the payment on my reality check

Today is Pablo Picasso's birthday
(October 25, 1881)
"I begin with an idea
and then it becomes
something else"

One Idea Can Change Your World

REALITY
What is..

Reality is a sublime comedy...
staged for your education and amusement
(Think of the world as a TV set... and you own the remote)

Today's Affirmation:

Curtain up...
you're on!!

Idea of the Day:

Since you can't *change* reality...
change the eyes which *see* reality

REDUNDANT
Quit Being..

Quit being
redundant

Today's Affirmation:

I quit being redundant

Idea of the Day:

REINCARNATION

Keep trying until
you get it right

Today's Affirmation:

If I were a flower, I would have been a carnation...
then in the next life, a carnation once again

Idea of the Day:

If you resist reincarnation
you will be forced to accept it in the next lifetime

"Ya'all come back real soon now, ya' hear?"

Today is Bill Gates' birthday
(October 28, 1955)
Bill Gates is one of the world's wealthiest men
as well as one of the world's most generous philanthropists:
"My success, part of it certainly is
that I have focused in
on a few things"

RELATIONSHIP
Secret Of A Good..

S W A M I S E Z

Spend each day as if it is
your first and last day
together

Today's Affirmation:

*I appreciate each and every day
of my relationship*

Idea of the Day:

Relationship is a mirror
into which our inner being gets reflected

RELAX
Why It's Okay To..

S W A M I   S E Z

You will know everything you need to know when you need to know it

(Feel yourself go with the flow and be blissed... rather than resist and insist)

Today's Affirmation:

I relax into the idea that I will know what I need to know when I need to know it (to achieve the max, I relax... relax... relax...)

Idea of the Day:

Enjoy the process... you'll get there soon enough

Today is Ruth Gordon's birthday
(October 30,1896)
" If you wanna' be high, be high
and if you wanna' be low, be low
there's a million ways to go
you know that there are"

RELIEF
How To Experience..

S   W   A   M   I   S   E   Z

Expand your belief...
and realize relief

Today's Affirmation:

Any remaining ghosts and goblins of fear,
as I so believe… they magically disappear

Idea of the Day:

It's October 31 st...
I believe I'll have another piece
of Halloween candy, please!

RIGHT
On Being..

S W A M I S E Z

Even a stopped clock is right twice a day

Today's Affirmation:

*I know what is right... when I "see the light"
and so I am inspired to write something " bright!! "*

Idea of the Day:

"Whether you think you can
or you think you can't... you're right"
— *Henry Ford*

If it takes morning, noon or night...
there's always time to do it right

SATISFACTION

S W A M I S E Z

"Always be satisfied
with the applause of your own conscience"
— *Arlene B. Gibson, J.D.*

Today's Affirmation:

*I find self-satisfaction
in doing good deeds of action*

Idea of the Day:

"There's more credit and satisfaction
in being a first-rate truck driver
than a tenth rate executive"
— *B.C. Forbes*

A little praise... goes a long ways

"Was it good for you?"

Reward yourself:
"Very good... very good...YAAY *!!*"
— *Laugh Yoga cheer*

SCHOOL
..Of Life

S   W   A   M   I   S   E   Z

Today is yesterday's pupil
(In the school of life, everyone is your teacher)

Today's Affirmation:
*I am a student in the school of life...
and I learn the steps to conquer every strife*

Idea of the Day:

You are not fully realized...
until you fully realize it

Today is Roseanne Barr's birthday
(November 3, 1952)
"Women complain about premenstrual syndrome
but I think of it as the only time of the month
I can be myself"

SEEING

All..

S W A M I S E Z

See it as it *is*...
and you will see yourself as you *are*

Today's Affirmation:

It IS what it is...
"Is 'R' Us"

Idea of the Day:

Today is Will Rogers' birthday
(November 4, 1879)
"Live in such a way that you would not be ashamed
to sell your parrot to the town gossip"

The Five Sense:
1. sight
2. smell
3. touch
4. horse
5. common

SEEK
..And Ye Shall Find

What you are looking for...
is looking for you

Today's Affirmation:

I ask and I receive, I seek and I find...
I knock and it is opened unto my mind

Idea of the Day:

The road to knowledge begins with the turn of the page

The moment you come to your own being
a revolution happens to your vision...
your whole outlook changes
and what you do, you do from joy

Once you discover your authentic self
you can embrace all aspects of the human experience
from the earthly to the most celestial

SELF TALK

Positive..

S W A M I S E Z

"Have I told you lately that I love you?"

Today's Affirmation:

*I love and accept myself...
just the way I am*

Idea of the Day:

"Crash through your shell of self-consciousness"
— *Dale Carnegie*

Listen to the silent voice of your soul...
as it knows what you need to be happy
(Beware the loud voice of the ego...
as it will glibly spout and drown all else out)

"The better part of happiness
is to wish to be what you are"
— *Desiderius Erasmus*

One Idea Can Change Your World

SERIOUS
Surely You Can't Be..

S W A M I   S E Z

I am serious...
(and don't call me Shirley!!)

Today's Affirmation:

I do not take anything too seriously...
(surely you jest!!)

Idea of the Day:

Laughter is useful
in combating the serious

Whatever the situation is...
find the humor in it

SINCERITY

S W A M I S E Z

Always be sincere...
whether you mean it or not

Today's Affirmation:

"Hey, I like your tie"

Idea of the Day:

SITUATIONS
How To Deal With New..

Just make it up
as you go

Today's Affirmation:

Today I trust my spontaneity

Idea of the Day:

<u>SMILE</u>
Increase Your Face Value

S W A M I S E Z

Everyone smiles
in the same language
(it takes 17 muscles to smile... and 43 to frown:
Exercise yourself happy!!)

Today's Affirmation:

I am not fully dressed...
without a smile expressed

Idea of the Day:

If you don't feel like smiling, fake it...
a smile flexes your zygomaticus
(smile muscle)
and improves well-being
and enhances a healthy immune system

SOLUTION
Ultimate Daily..

S W A M I S E Z

Have a
nice day
(Dare to think the opposite of your problem)

Today's Affirmation:
Today, in spite of what may get in the way...
I wholeheartedly enjoy my day

Idea of the Day:

Knowledge of what is possible
is the beginning of happiness

Where there's a will...
there's a way

SPILLED MILK

Crying Over..

S   W   A   M   I   S   E   Z

Quit crying over spilled milk...
If the cat hasn't licked it up by now,
it's probably spoiled anyway

T o d a y ' s   A f f i r m a t i o n :

Like they say in New Jersey:
"Fuhgedaboudit!"

I d e a   o f   t h e   D a y :

Pete Best,
who was kicked out of the Beatles and replaced by Ringo Starr
after 40 years of bitterness and depression declared in 2006:
" I was strong enough to put it behind me...
You wake up one morning and say
'What's the use of crying over spilled milk?'"

Spilled milk?
Milk another cow !!

*(we're milking this one
for all it's worth !!)*

STAND
Taking A..

S W A M I S E Z

If you don't stand for something...
you'll fall for anything

Today's Affirmation:

I lend a hand....
and take a stand

Idea of the Day:

STRUGGLE
Key To Releasing..

S W A M I S E Z

Release struggle... in favor of snuggle
(Surrender your self-centered self...
and birth your *expanded* spiritual self)

Today's Affirmation:

*I allow love
to help me overcome all problems*

Idea of the Day:

Life is an endless struggle
full of frustrations and challenges...
but eventually you find a
hair stylist you like

*When in Palm Springs...
visit
"PS I Love Your Hair"
(Tell 'em "Swami sent you")*

Today is Prince Charles' birthday
(November 14, 1948)
"I learned the way a monkey learns...
by watching its parents"

STUPID
Fixing..

You can't fix stupid
(Are you swimming in the shallow end of the thinking pool??)

Today's Affirmation:

*I do my part...
to do things smart*

Idea of the Day:

"Everyone is ignorant... only on different subjects"
— *Will Rogers*

So, if ignorance is bliss... why aren't more people happy?

"Stupid is as stupid does..."
— *Forrest Gump*
... like asking for a price check a the 99 Cent Store
... like taking your shoes off to count to 20
... like inventing an inflatable dart board
... like ordering your sushi well done
... like selling the car for gas money

*... and what about the nearsighted snake
who meets up with a plate of spaghetti
and thought he was at an orgy*

SUCCEEDING
Keys To..

S W A M I S E Z

Associate with
your level *and above*

Today's Affirmation:

I know that birds of a feather flock together...
and I am an eagle

Idea of the Day:

"Success is a state of mind...
If you want success, start thinking of yourself as a success"
— Joyce Brothers

"To laugh often and much...
to leave the world a bit better
to know even one life has breathed easier
because you have lived...
that is to have succeeded"
— Ralph Waldo Emerson

Live well...
Laugh often
Love much

One Idea Can Change Your World

SVCCESS
Formula For..

Success comes to those
who dare to begin
(Results are the extension... of conscious intention)

Today's Affirmation:

I have a life of action, a will to accomplish, and a joy for what is true
I pursue that which I can be... the best at what I do

Idea of the Day:

The more successful I am...the more the world will benefit

Four Steps to Business Success:
1. Find out what they want
2. Get it for them
3. Get paid
4. Send them a Christmas card

Swami tips:
1. You can never lose money making a profit
2. Always count up from zero
3. Never count down from "coulda' been"

SUCCESS
Maximizing Mileage

S W A M I S E Z

One of the most important principles of success
is developing the habit of
going the extra mile

Today's Affirmation:
I agree with John D. Rockefeller
that
"the secret to success is to do common things uncommonly well"

Idea of the Day:

Success is getting what you want...
Happiness is wanting what you get

Go the extra m i l e ... it's never too crowded

SUNSHINE

Being..

S W A M I S E Z

Let the first thing you say...
brighten everyone's day!!

Today's Affirmation:

*I speak only good...
and brighten up the neighborhood*

Idea of the Day:

"A single sunbeam is enough
to drive away many shadows"
— Saint Francis of Assisi

Offer and accept a helping hand...
we are in this together

THINKING
Changing Your..

S W A M I   S E Z

If you keep thinking what you've always thought... you'll keep getting what you always got
("Change your thinking... change your life")

Today's Affirmation:

As I steer the course of my thinking...
I keep my "ship of life" from sinking

Idea of the Day:

You are the creator of your own thoughts:
Energy follows thought... you actually become what you think

THINK IT... BE IT... DO IT

When you have unwanted thoughts, words or images
about what you *do not* want...
Just say "*Cancel, cancel, cancel*"

Bring yourself to the state of pure nothingness
and focus on your breath and this moment now

Then say, "Thank you, Thought...
I've received your message
now I let you go"

Words forming thought and visa versa

One Idea Can Change Your World

THOUGHTS

Be careful of your thoughts...
they may become words at any moment
(Ever stop to think... and then forget to start again?)

Today's Affirmation:

I am the master of my own thoughts

Idea of the Day:

Concentrated thoughts produce desired results

"Our life depends on what our thoughts make it"
—*Marcus Aurelius*

Thoughts lead to belief
which leads to attitude
which leads to feeling
which leads to outcome
which leads to...
another thought

How much deeper would the ocean be
if sponges didn't live there?

Today is Voltaire's birthday
(November 21, 1694)
"Love truth and pardon error"

One Idea Can Change Your World

THRILLS
Cheap..

Let's just pop a few dozen yards of bubble wrap and call it a day

Today's Affirmation:

*I am easily amused and can find joy
in the simplest of activities*

Idea of the Day:

...and if you don't have any bubble wrap
you can always squeeze a loaf of Wonder Bread
into a pasty dough ball

TIME
Constructive Use Of..

Major score...
clean a drawer

Today's Affirmation:

When I take time to organize my "stuff..."
I feel in balance, and have more than time enough

Idea of the Day:

It's really time to clean your room
when there's more on the floor... than in the drawer

"Time flies like an arrow... fruit flies like a banana"
— *Groucho Marx*

"Time's fun when you're having flies"
— *Kermit the Frog*

TIME
Perspective

In just two days...
tomorrow will be yesterday
(Time is nature's way of keeping everything from happening all at once...
Warning: dates in calendar are closer than they appear)

Today's Affirmation:

Time is relative
(depending on which relative I am spending time with)

Idea of the Day:

Time has no meaning in the face of creativity

Today is Dale Carnegie's birthday
(November 24 1888)
"All of us tend to put off living...
we are all dreaming of some
magical rose garden over the horizon
instead of enjoying the roses that are blooming
outside our windows today"

TODAY
Value Of..

S W A M I S E Z

"One today is worth two tomorrows"
— *Benjamin Franklin*

Today's Affirmation:

I appreciate the ever present now

Idea of the Day:

The day after tomorrow is the third day of the rest of your life

You can never be where you have been...
so wherever you are
is one step further along the path
than wherever you were

One Idea Can Change Your World

TODAY

..Yesterday And Tomorrow

S W A M I S E Z

Cherish your yesterdays... dream your tomorrows
and live your todays
(Today is the tomorrow you worried about yesterday)

Today's Affirmation:

Yesterday, today and tomorrow all have their place...
I can only live today in happiness and grace

Idea of the Day:

One Idea Can Change Your World

TODAY AND TOMORROW

A "Seussian" View

S W A M I S E Z

"Today was good, today was fun
Tomorrow is another one"
— *Dr. Seuss*

Today's Affirmation:

*I find joy and wisdom
in my favorite classic childhood books*

Idea of the Day:

Don't put off 'til tomorrow
what you can get someone else
to do today

TOMORROW

Faith In..

After all...
"Tomorrow *IS* another day"
— Scarlett O'Hara
Gone With the Wind

Today's Affirmation:

I am inspired by famous quotes from my favorite movies

Idea of the Day:

Today is Jon Stewart's birthday
(November 28, 1965)
"As long as I don't end up hosting a
skin care commercial with Cher, I'm happy"

One Idea Can Change Your World

TOMORROW
Preparing For..

The only preparation for tomorrow...
is the right use of today

Today's Affirmation:

*I know that today is yesterday's effect...
and tomorrow's cause*

Idea of the Day:

Change your thinking... change your life

THE JOURNEY IS THE DESTINATION

TOMORROW
The Promise Of..

Tomorrow holds promises
today could not fulfill

Today's Affirmation:

*I know what does not fit in today...
can easily fit in tomorrow*

Idea of the Day:

Today is Winston Churchill's birthday
(November 30, 1874)
"Never hold discussions with the monkey...
when the organ grinder is in the room"

TRAIN OF THOUGHT

If You Lose Your..

S W A M I S E Z

Go by plane !!

(see things from a new perspective)

Today's Affirmation:

To expand my understanding of any objective...
I see my situation from many a perspective

Idea of the Day:

Two wrongs don't make a right...
but two Wrights made an airplane

<u>TRASH</u>
Let's Hear It For..

S W A M I S E Z

Every day...
throw something away
(When in doubt... throw it out)

Today's Affirmation:

*I organize and clean my "stuff" up easily
to keep my mind and work space clutter-free*

Idea of the Day:

"Out of clutter... find simplicity"
— *Albert Einstein*

TRANQUILITY

Domestic..

S W A M I S E Z

No man has ever been shot while washing the dishes

Today's Affirmation:

When I help my mate...
I truly rate!!

Idea of the Day:

DECEMBER 4

TRUST
What To..

Trust your
original thought

Today's Affirmation:

*I realize that my first thought...
is probably my best thought*

Idea of the Day:

"Trust everybody... but cut the cards"
— Folk wisdom of the Old West

TRVTH
Arguing With The..

You can't argue with the truth... true or true?
— *Mitchell J. Santell*

(Ye shall know the truth and the truth shall make you free)
— *John 8:32*

Today's Affirmation:

I speak the truth... and the truth sets me free
The truth needs no memory

Idea of the Day:

Seek what is good and what is true... that is all you need to do

Today is Little Richard's birthday
(December 5, 1932)
"A wop bop a loo mop a lop bam boom!"

Little Richard traded the blues
to become the architect of rock 'n' roll

TRUTH
The Naked..

"Spin" must have clothes...
but truth loves to go naked
(Humor is truth... with a little curlicue at the end)

Today's Affirmation:

The words I speak, I "spin" not...
because the truth speaks for itself, as it ought

Idea of the Day:

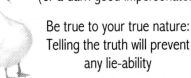

If it looks like a duck
walks like a duck
and quacks like a duck
its a duck
(or a darn good impersonator)

Be true to your true nature:
Telling the truth will prevent
any lie-ability

Remember, if you tell the truth
you don't have to remember anything

One Idea Can Change Your World

UNDERSTANDING

If you don't understand...
perhaps you over sit

For maximum traction...
I take appropriate action

Idea of the Day:

"All that we are
is the result of what we have thought"
— *Buddha*

"Horse sense is the thing a horse has
which keeps it from betting on people"
— *W. C. Fields*

UNITY
(Goo Goo Ga Joob)

S W A M I   S E Z

"I am you... as you are me...
as we are all together"
—*The Beatles*
'I am the Walrus'

Today's Affirmation:

*I realize that we are
all in this together*

Idea of the Day:

"Love is a mysterious divine glue that unites the hearts of all"
—*Sivananda*

On the great *wheel of life*... each of us is a *spokes*person

"When spiders web unite... they can tie up a lion"
—*Ethiopian proverb*

Today is Flip Wilson's birthday
(December 8, 1933)
"What you see is what you get"

<u>UNIVERSE</u>
In Flow With The..

Are you diagonally parked in a Parallel Universe?

Reach out for what you want and the Universe reaches out and meets you half way

Today's Affirmation:

My soul greets the soul of the Universe through everyone I meet and I am totally in flow... everywhere I go

Idea of the Day:

The Universe is a teaching machine... teaching what works

Right now the Universe is conspiring to make you happy...
and there's nothing you can do about it

When it comes to the ultimate test...
the Universe knows best

Today is Emmet Kelly's birthday
(December 9, 1898)
"By laughing at me, the audience really
laughs at themselves, and realizing they have done this
gives them sort of a spiritual second wind
for going back into the battles of life"

One Idea Can Change Your World

UPHOLSTERY MACHINE

Falling Into An..

S W A M I   S E Z

You are
fully recovered

Today's Affirmation:

Today I am fully recovered

Idea of the Day:

VEIL
Piercing The..

S W A M I S E Z

Pierce the veil of illusion...
Hey, wait a minute, those are my good curtains *!!*

Today's Affirmation:
*I pierce the veil of illusion...
and I see clearly — no confusion*

Idea of the Day:

Since there is nothing large or small to the Infinite...
there is nothing in your experience beyond its action

VICTORIA'S SECRET

Less is more

Today's Affirmation:

I realize that
less is more... more or less

Idea of the Day:

Today is Frank Sinatra's birthday
(December 12, 1915)
"To think I did all that
and may I say, not in a shy way
oh no, oh no not me... I did it my way"

One Idea Can Change Your World

WALDO
Beyond Where's..

Go
find
YOURSELF!!

Today's Affirmation:

*My problem is like a puzzle...
that I readily solve*

Idea of the Day:

WASTING TIME

There is no more time to waste...
Put this book down
and go *DO* something*!!*

Today's Affirmation:

I realize I have places to be and people to see...
Busy me !!

Idea of the Day:

Today is Nostradamus' birthday
(December 14, 1503)
Most of the 942 prophetic verses of Nostradamus
were in the form of a quatrain:
to see the future, get on a "higher plane"
or go by "train"

WEEKEND
..Happiness

S W A M I S E Z

You know it's been a good weekend
when you pass the want ads in the Sunday paper...
and go directly to the comic section

Today's Affirmation:

I start my day reading the comic section first

Idea of the Day:

One Idea Can Change Your World

WHAT KIND OF FOOL
..Am I

S W A M I S E Z

Fool me once, shame on you
Fool me twice, shame on me
Fool me three times...I must like it!

Today's Affirmation:

I am wise, aware and cool...
and play not the role of the fool

Idea of the Day:

Today is Sir Arthur C. Clarke's birthday
(December 16,1917)
Clarke's epitaph for himself:
"He never grew up, but he never stopped growing"

WHO AM I ??

S   W   A   M   I   S   E   Z

"I am all that was, that is and all that shall be"

—A creed of Beethoven,
framed and kept permanently on his desk

Today's Affirmation:

I, like Beethoven
am all that

Idea of the Day:

You do not need to add anything to yourself
in order to be yourself fully

Today is Ludwig van Beethoven's birthday
(December 17, 1770)

Turn your *malady* into a *melody*

One Idea Can Change Your World

WHOLENESS
Like Golf

S W A M I   S E Z

You are one, you are whole...
you are a whole in one
('scuse me, I'm off to the 19th hole)

Today's Affirmation:

I am whole, I am one...I am a whole in one

Idea of the Day:

Today is Keith Richard's birthday
(December 18,1943)
"You can't always get what you want
but if you try some time, you just might find
you get what you need"

One Idea Can Change Your World

WHOSE DAY

..Is It Anyway?!

S W A M I S E Z

No one can run your day...
without your permission

Today's Affirmation:

I am in charge of my day

Idea of the Day:

WHY?

"Why not ??"
— *Timothy Leary*
(last words)

Today's Affirmation:

My "because" is guided
by my inner vision

Idea of the Day:

WINNERS

Winners are grinners
Smile and the world smiles with you:
The will to win... is the courage to begin

Today's Affirmation:

"I am good, great and grand... right here and now where I stand
Knowing I am a winner... makes me a grinner" – Bro. Joseph Leavell

Idea of the Day:

You can be a w i n n e r !!
(see contest details page 369)

Today is Frank Zappa's birthday
(December 21, 1937)
"Never stop until your good becomes better
and your better becomes the best"

WISDOM
Milk Of Human..

S W A M I S E Z

Got Swami?

---✹---

Today's Affirmation:

I gladly trade all my blues for some "hot-out-of-the-oven" brownies...
(see Swami Brownie Recipe on page 368)

Idea of the Day:

The sage is guided by what he feels...
and not by what he sees

Endeavor to be healthy, wealthy and wise

Some folks are wise... and some are otherwise

"Knowledge speaks... but wisdom listens"
— *Jimi Hendrix*

"En boca cerrada... no entran moscas"
(a closed mouth... gathers no flies)
— *Grandma Maria Galante*

One Idea Can Change Your World

WITHIN

Going..

If you don't go within...
you go without

Today's Affirmation:

I begin...
by going within

Idea of the Day:

Silence is golden...
get rich quick!

Stillness can be the most powerful action of all

Gee(G), you(U) are(R) you(U)
You are your own guru

There is no guru
who knows more than you do

DECEMBER 24

<u>WORD</u>
Integrity of your..

S W A M I S E Z

If you wouldn't write it and sign it...
don't say it*!!*
(P.S. Today is Swami's birthday...tomorrow is Jesus')

Today's Affirmation:
*The words I use to express myself...
are the seeds of my future experience*

Idea of the Day:

Swami Sez:
"LAUGH AND BE HAPPY AND BE HERE NOW...
(or as soon as you can!)"

One Idea Can Change Your World

©2006 Church of Truth Through Humor / Swami Sez Press / B.E.Singer. All Rights Reserved

<u>WORDS</u>
..And Ideas

S W A M I S E Z

Your words are pegs to hang ideas on...
use them wisely
(words without ideas are like sails without wind)

Today's Affirmation:

My ideas are made manifest through my words, which I use wisely
(Speaking of wise men, it's Christmas Day... Happy Birthday, Jesus!)

Idea of the Day:

Today is Carlos Castanada's birthday
(December 25 1925)
"Do you know at this very moment you are surrounded by eternity
and that you can use that eternity if you so desire?"

WORK
..And Luck

S W A M I   S E Z

The harder you work...
the more luck you will have

Today's Affirmation:

I work with diligence and pluck...
and am grateful for my luck

Idea of the Day:

If you choose a job that you like
you will never have to work a day in your life

The more you can reduce the gap between
who you are and what you do...
the more effortless your work will become

It's December 26th ...
"Free Christmas Trees for all my friends !!"

One Idea Can Change Your World

WORK/LOVE/DANCE

Work like you don't need the money,
love like you've never been hurt,
and dance like nobody is watching

— *Mark Twain*

Today's Affirmation:

I work, love and dance...
with free abandon

Idea of the Day:

WORRY

S W A M I   S E Z

Worry brings tomorrow's clouds over today's sunshine

Today's Affirmation:

*If I feel "the worries" coming on, and I start to "feel crappy..."
I start singing the song, "Don't Worry, Be Happy"*

Idea of the Day:

"Since *everything* is matter... *nothing* matters"
— *A Course in Miracles*

Worry is the interest paid on trouble before it falls due:

95% of what you worry about will never happen anyway
*(the other 5% will keep you so busy
you won't have time to worry)*

WORTH
Your True..

SWAMI SEZ

Your dreams minus your doubts equals your true worth

Today's Affirmation:

I follow my dreams with elation... passion, joy and determination

Idea of the Day:

One Idea Can Change Your World

YOU
..Are Loved

S W A M I S E Z

If God had a refrigerator...
your picture would be on it

Today's Affirmation:

I am loved

Idea of the Day:

You are the only you who ever was... and ever will be
(You are rarer than the rarest diamond)

ZEN
Finding..

S W A M I S E Z

The zen you find at the top of a mountain...
is the zen you bring up there with you

Today's Affirmation:

*Today is New Year's Eve... I stand at the top of the mountain
and look out to the vista of a clear new year*

Idea of the Day:

The End Signifies a New Beginning...

Much Bliss
and
Many Blessings
To You *!!*

Celebrate Life Everlaughing!!!

If you overcame "the blues" (or a state of depression) by using this book
Congratulations !! You did it your self !!! (Glad I could help) Love to hear from you...
You can e-mail me at: SwamiSezPress@gmail.com

One Idea Can Change Your World

Swami Sez:

Remember…
A Good Hearty
Laugh Is Worth
Ten Thousand
Groans

Whatever It Is,
Let It Go…
And Know That
"This Too Shall Pass"

Focus on the Positive

Love and Serve Others
If It Is To Be…It Is Up To Me
Act As Though...It Is Already So
Do the Right Thing
Harm No One
Keep Your Agreements
Don't Take It Personally

Choose to Lose the Blues
Nothing is Permanent
Except Change

Be Here Now…
(Or as Soon as You Can)

Laugh and Be Happy!!

Many Blessings to You,

Swami Sez

Mrs. Swami's Brownie Recipe

Mrs. Swami says:
"Why re-invent the wheel?"

Fortunately, a confirmed
"Brownie-aholic" (Lindsay Frucci) founded a company
that makes the very excellent
NO-PUDGE
Decadent Fudgy and Chewy Fudge Brownie Mix

You can pick up a box of this
world famous brownie mix
at your local Health Food Store or Grocery Market…
Look for a pink and white box:
you can't miss it!!

To
"s w a m i t i z e:"
Mrs. Swami suggests any combination of the following:

An extra 2 tablespoons of Vanilla
Candied Nuts (pecans or walnuts)
½ cup Morello Cherries (drained thoroughly and minced)
Chocolate Chips

Exquisitely delicious!!!

One bite…
and you'll *surely* be willing
to
"trade the blues for brownies!!!!"

Got milk?

Swami Sez:

"That's A Great Idea"
CONTEST!!

WIN
A DAY AT DISNEYLAND
"The Happiest Place on Earth"

A "Ticket for You" or "Tickets for Two"

TO ENTER:
go to www.SwamiSez.com
Tell us one of your
"IDEAS OF THE DAY"
that you wrote down in your
Swami Sez
Trade the Blues for Brownies
'Idea of the Day' Journal

Write a brief paragraph (or a complete story)
about the positive outcome
you experienced as a result of your idea.
Include how the result of this idea positively
did one or more of the following:
    a) changed *your* life
    b) changed *another's* life
    c) changed the world

Winner need not be present to win*

* Remember, today is the *gift*…
that is why they call it the *present*

Good Luck !!

This prize is awarded every Christmas Eve for as long as this book is actively published

LAUGH YOURSELF WELL

Presented to you in the spirit of Norman Cousins, who checked out of a hospital and into a hotel room to *laugh himself well* by watching and laughing at funny movies (especially lots of Charlie Chaplin, Marx Brothers, and classic Candid Camera).

Here then are:

The Top 100 All Time Funniest Comedy Motion Pictures
according to the American Film Institute (AFI)

Swami Sez: go to your local video store and check out any of these movies and "laugh yourself silly!"

Laughter IS the best medicine !!!

1. SOME LIKE IT HOT (1959)
2. TOOTSIE (1982)
3. DR. STRANGELOVE (1964)
4. ANNIE HALL (1977)
5. DUCK SOUP (1933)
6. BLAZING SADDLES (1974)
7. M*A*S*H (1970)
8. IT HAPPENED ONE NIGHT (1934)
9. THE GRADUATE (1967)
10. AIRPLANE! (1980)
11. THE PRODUCERS (1968)
12. A NIGHT AT THE OPERA (1935)
13. YOUNG FRANKENSTEIN (1974)
14. BRINGING UP BABY (1938)
15. THE PHILADELPHIA STORY (1940)
16. SINGIN' IN THE RAIN (1952)
17. THE ODD COUPLE (1968)
18. THE GENERAL (1927)
19. HIS GIRL FRIDAY (1940)
20. THE APARTMENT (1960)
21. A FISH CALLED WANDA (1988)
22. ADAM'S RIB (1949)
23. WHEN HARRY MET SALLY... (1989)
24. BORN YESTERDAY (1950)
25. THE GOLD RUSH (1925)
26. BEING THERE (1979)
27. THERE'S SOMETHING ABOUT MARY (1998)
28. GHOSTBUSTERS (1984)
29. THIS IS SPINAL TAP (1984)
30. ARSENIC AND OLD LACE (1944)
31. RAISING ARIZONA (1987)
32. THE THIN MAN (1934)
33. MODERN TIMES (1936)
34. GROUNDHOG DAY (1993)
35. HARVEY (1950)
36. NATIONAL LAMPOON'S ANIMAL HOUSE (1978)
37. THE GREAT DICTATOR (1940)
38. CITY LIGHTS (1931)
39. SULLIVAN'S TRAVELS (1941)
40. IT'S A MAD MAD MAD MAD WORLD (1963)

41. MOONSTRUCK (1987)
42. BIG (1988)
43. AMERICAN GRAFFITI (1973)
44. MY MAN GODFREY (1936)
45. HAROLD AND MAUDE (1972)
46. MANHATTAN (1979)
47. SHAMPOO (1975)
48. A SHOT IN THE DARK (1964)
49. TO BE OR NOT TO BE (1942)
50. CAT BALLOU (1965)
51. THE SEVEN YEAR ITCH (1955)
52. NINOTCHKA (1939)
53. ARTHUR (1981)
54. THE MIRACLE OF MORGAN'S CREEK (1944)
55. THE LADY EVE (1941)
56. ABBOTT AND COSTELLO MEET FRANKENSTEIN (1948)
57. DINER (1982)
58. IT'S A GIFT (1934)
59. A DAY AT THE RACES (1937)
60. TOPPER (1937)
61. WHAT'S UP, DOC? (1972)
62. SHERLOCK, JR. (1924)
63. BEVERLY HILLS COP (1984)
64. BROADCAST NEWS (1987)
65. HORSE FEATHERS (1932)
66. TAKE THE MONEY AND RUN (1969)
67. MRS. DOUBTFIRE (1993)
68. THE AWFUL TRUTH (1937)
69. BANANAS (1971)
70. MR. DEEDS GOES TO TOWN (1936)
71. CADDYSHACK (1980)
72. MR. BLANDINGS BUILDS HIS DREAM HOUSE (1948)
73. MONKEY BUSINESS (1931)
74. 9 TO 5 (1980)
75. SHE DONE HIM WRONG (1933)
76. VICTOR/VICTORIA (1982)
77. THE PALM BEACH STORY (1942)
78. ROAD TO MOROCCO (1942)
79. THE FRESHMAN (1925)
80. SLEEPER (1973)
81. THE NAVIGATOR (1924)
82. PRIVATE BENJAMIN (1980)
83. FATHER OF THE BRIDE (1950)
84. LOST IN AMERICA (1985)
85. DINNER AT EIGHT (1933)
86. CITY SLICKERS (1991)
87. FAST TIMES AT RIDGEMONT HIGH (1982)
88. BEETLEJUICE (1988)
89. THE JERK (1979)
90. WOMAN OF THE YEAR (1942)
91. THE HEARTBREAK KID (1972)
92. BALL OF FIRE (1941)
93. FARGO (1996)
94. AUNTIE MAME (1958)
95. SILVER STREAK (1976)
96. SONS OF THE DESERT (1933)
97. BULL DURHAM (1988)
98. THE COURT JESTER (1956)
99. NUTTY PROFESSOR (1963)
100. GOOD MORNING, VIETNAM (1987)

LAUGH AT THE FUNNIEST

Comedy Central's 100 Greatest Stand Up Comedians of All Time

Hey, where's Carrot Top???

1. Richard Pryor
2. George Carlin
3. Lenny Bruce
4. Woody Allen
5. Chris Rock
6. Steve Martin
7. Rodney Dangerfield
8. Bill Cosby
9. Roseanne Barr
10. Eddie Murphy
11. Johnny Carson
12. Jerry Seinfeld
13. Robin Williams
14. Bob Newhart
15. David Letterman
16. Ellen Degeneres
17. Don Rickles
18. Jonathan Winters
19. Bill Hicks
20. Sam Kinison
21. Dennis Miller
22. Robert Klein
23. Steven Wright
24. Redd Foxx
25. Bob Hope
26. Ray Romano
27. Jay Leno
28. Jack Benny
29. Mlton Berle
30. Garry Shandling
31. George Burns
32. Albert Brooks
33. Andy Kaufman

34. Buddy Hackett
35. Phyllis Diller
36. Jim Carrey
37. Martin Lawrence
38. Bill Maher
39. Billy Crystal
40. Mort Sahl
41. Jon Stewart
42. Flip Wilson
43. Dave Chappelle
44. Joan Rivers
45. Richard Lewis
46. Adam Sandler
47. Henny Youngman
48. Tim Allen
49. Freddie Prinze
50. Denis Leary
51. Lewis Black
52. Damon Wayons
53. David Brenner
54. D.L. Hughley
55. Alan King
56. Colin Quinn
57. Richard Jeni
58. Larry Miller
59. Gilbert Gottfried
60. Jeff Foxworthy
61. Bobcat Goldthwait
62. Eddie Griffin
63. Jackie Mason
64. Richard Belzer
65. Sinbad
66. Shelley Burman

67. Kevin Pollack
68. Dave Attel
69. Pat Cooper
70. Wanda Sykes
71. Red Buttons
72. Bernie Mac
73. Elaine Boosler
74. Paul Rodriguez
75. Eddie Izzard
76. Robert Schimmel
77. Paul Reiser
78. Cedric the Entrtnr
79. Dom Irerra
80. Bobby Slayton
81. Dick Gregory
82. Howie Mandel
83. Norm McDonald
84. Drew Carey
85. David Cross
86. Jay Mohr
87. Brett Butler
88. Paula Poundstone
89. Kevin James
90. Dana Carvey
91. Jim Breuer
92. Louie Anderson
93. George Wallace
94. David Allen Grier
95. Andrew Dice Clay
96. Joey Bishop
97. Sandra Bernhard
98. Louis C.K.
99. Janeane Garofalo
100. Gallagher

SWAMI SEZ

GET THINGS DONE:

Om / Chant
3 Times:
"Holeeee Shmoleeee!!!"

Now
Chant:
*"Ohhh, Ohhh . . . Ask Patty"**

Then
If Patty's
Not Available . . .

You Gotta'
*DO IT
YOURSELF!!!*

* *"Om Mani Padme Om"*
  (which means "the pearl is within the oyster")
  is also a very good one

Humor Lover?
Visit Swami on the Net:
www.SwamiSez.com

Swami Sez:

HIERARCHY OF NEEDS
(with thanks to Abraham Maslow)

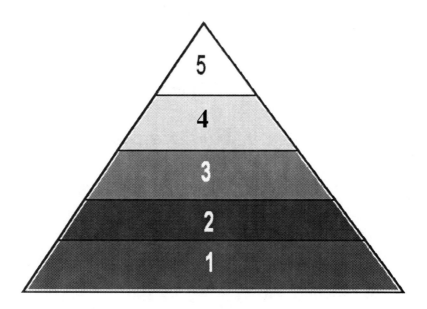

1) PHYSIOLOGICAL ("Me so hungry / Me so horny")

2) SAFETY ("Look both ways before crossing")

3) LOVE / BELONGING ("All you need is love" *The Beatles*)

4) STATUS / ESTEEM ("A Rolls Royce and two bottles of Dom Perignon, please")

5) READ ALL SWAMI SEZ BOOKS ("Actualization")

Laugh some more at:
www.SwamiSez.com

Church of Truth Through Humor™

THE 7 COMMANDMENTS
... (AND 3 SUGGESTIONS)

I. NEVER TELL A JOKE IF YOU CAN'T REMEMBER THE PUNCH LINE.

II. A HALF TRUTH IS A WHOLE LIE.

III. DO THE RIGHT THING, HARM NO ONE, AND KEEP YOUR AGREEMENTS.

IV. CAPERS ARE NOT A NECESSARY INGREDIENT FOR LOX AND BAGELS. HOWEVER, IF THERE'S SMOKE, THERE'S PROBABLY SMOKED SALMON.

V. IF YOU GO AWAY FROM THE TABLE HUNGRY ... IT'S YOUR OWN FAULT.

VI. PRACTICE RANDOM ACTS OF KINDNESS ... EVERY DAY.

VII. TAKE TIME TO SMELL THE ROSES ALONG THE WAY.

THE 3 SUGGESTIONS

VIII. MEN: PUT THE TOILET SEAT DOWN AFTER YOU ARE FINISHED.

IX WOMEN: YOU DID NOT SAVE MORE MONEY THAN YOU SPENT IF YOU BOUGHT A THOUSAND DOLLAR DRESS FOR $450.
(Regarding #8 above, if you *really* loved your man, you would put the toilet seat *up* after you were finished.)

X WHY CAN'T WE ALL JUST GET ALONG ???

11TH COMMANDMENT
YOU MAY NOT SAY, "MAY I MAKE A SUGGESTION ..." UNLESS IT'S A REALLY GOOD ONE.

BASIC TENET:
LEAD US NOT INTO TEMPTATION ... *and deliver us a pizza !!!*
Official Exercise: *Humorobics*
Patron Saint: *Our Lady of Perpetual Humor*
Constant Improvement: *'3-minute Abs!!'*

Attend Services on the Net at www.churchoftruththroughhumor.org

Swami Sez...

...is the alter ego and satire / parody / wisdom persona of Bruce E. Singer, Humorist, Author, Entertainer, Composer/Songwriter and Voting Grammy Member.

As an entertainer, he performed in the original "Legends of Rock 'n' Roll Shows," impersonating Little Richard, Ray Charles, Fats Domino, Sam the Sham & the Pharaohs and Cat Stevens (ah, the magic of makeup), being the warm up act for B.B. King, Tower of Power and Billy Preston.

The author credits the mentorship of his spiritual knowledge to the study of the Great Masters and every motivational seminar from Wayne Dyer to Tony Robbins and beyond.

Crediting his comedy skills to his teacher of a Hollywood Comedy Class in the 70's, "Swami's" comedic mentor and teacher was then-struggling comic, Jay Leno.

Photo Credit: Kathleen Clark Photography of Laguna Beach…Thanks, Katie!
Stylist: Kathleen Hanlen Singer… Thanks, Kathleen!

Printed in the United States
70562LV00001B/52